BECOMING A
HOLLOW
BONE

BECOMING A
HOLLOW
BONE

Responding to the
Call of
Our Ancestral Blood

ANNE WILSON SCHAEF

**COUNCIL
OAK
BOOKS**

Chicago

Copyright © 2013 by Anne Wilson Schaef
First hardcover edition published 2013
This edition published in 2021 by Council Oak Books
An imprint of Chicago Review Press Incorporated
814 North Franklin Street
Chicago, Illinois 60610
ISBN 978-1-64160-511-3

Every effort has been made to contact copyright holders and students for permission to reproduce borrowed material. We regret any oversights that may have occurred and will be pleased to rectify them in subsequent reprints of the work.

Library of Congress Cataloging-in-Publication Data is available from the Library of Congress

Cover design: Blue Design, Portland, Maine (www.bluedes.com)
Typesetting: Nord Compo

Printed in the United States of America

To my ancestors and all the elders who have taken it upon themselves to help me: remember that there is another way to walk on and interact with this earth and all its inhabitants—plant, animal, air, earth, and water. This way is gentle, spiritual, peaceful, and lives in wholeness.

Especially to Frank Fools Crow, the great Lakota Spiritual Leader, and to my great-grandmother, Mary Elizabeth Reed, a powerful yet gentle Tsa La Gi medicine woman. Both of whom are always by my side.

To all those living now and in the generations to come that know that we can live in peace and harmony with the earth, one another, and all creation.

We have not forgotten what must not be forgotten.

Contents

Author's Note   xi

Introduction.   1
The Beginning.   23
The First Process: The Sacred/Spiritual   27
The Second Process: Honoring Elders and Children   31
The Third Process: Participating in the Wholeness   39
The Fourth Process: All Is Relationship   44
The Fifth Process: Honor and Respect.   58
The Sixth Process: Nature   65
The Seventh Process: Process and Participation   72
The Eighth Process: Honesty.   77
The Ninth Process: The Process of Co-Creating   81
The Tenth Process: Valuing Differences.   85
The Eleventh Process: Being of Service.   91
The Twelfth Process: Living in Our Bodies and
    Taking Care of Them.   96
The Thirteenth Process: Listening and Humor 101
The Fourteenth Process: Living in Context—Don't Waste,
    Don't Abuse. 110
The Fifteenth Process: Science 114
The Sixteenth Process: Thinking 126
The Seventeenth Process: Patience 138
The Eighteenth Process: Humility 143

The Nineteenth Process: Prayer 147

The Twentieth Process: The Unseen 153

The Twenty-First Process: Living in Balance 166

In Summary: Creating a Wholeness of Being 173

Acknowledgments 177

"I am opening my heart to speak to you. Open yours to receive my words."

—Como

Author's Note

THERE ARE SEVERAL THINGS I want to say to you, my readers.

A. Everything in this book is true, personal, and what has been given me to share with you.

B. You may find some language forms that feel unfamiliar to you like the use of "and" instead of "but." Please let your mind struggle with this form if it is unfamiliar to you. We need to shake off the reductionism of our minds by the dominant culture and expand them like those of our ancestors. The use of "and" pushes us toward wholeness and is a start.

C. For those of you who have read my books in the past—

I know that I have not published a new book in a while. It's not that I have not been writing. I have—poetry, short stories, novels, screenplays, and, of course, nonfiction.

I just needed to retreat from the media, and the workshop/speech circuit, be quiet, and get grounded in my deepest truths and get clear on what I believe my Creator requires of me at this time. This book has come out of that time of retreat and there is more to come.

Thank you all for being patient with me as I have opened myself to new depths of sharing.

—Anne Wilson Schaef

Introduction

I RECENTLY MET WITH A GROUP OF PEOPLE, men and women, from all walks of life and several countries, some of whom:

1) *Knew* they had Native blood and were raised completely in a white world.

2) Thought they *did* have Native blood and were raised in a white world.

3) Thought they *might* have Native blood and were raised in a white world.

4) Had little clue about the specifics of their ancestry or having any Native blood, did not believe that they had any, and had always felt that they a) did not belong, b) were on the outside looking in, c) must have something wrong with them, d) much of the time believed the world around them was "crazy," and e) did not affirm their innate "knowings" and the thoughts, beliefs, and experiences that were most precious to them.

I have also met many people who:

1) Hated the color of their skin and were ashamed of their heritage.

2) Did not want to know if they were of Native blood.

3) Had families who had "passed" for white, and that was good enough for them.

4) Did not have the desire or energy to deal with having Native blood.

Most, if not all, of the above groups of people have deep-seated feelings of anger, alienation, frustration, and loneliness. These people often mistrust and deny their "knowings" and "awarenesses" with the result that they try to shut off their deep spiritual pain through addictions and behavioral problems. They have feelings of being "crazy," or suffer from psychoses, thoughts of suicide, or impulses toward violence.

As I listened to the individuals in this group share their feelings, experiences, and stories, I was reminded of a story shared with me by a Tsa La Gi (Cherokee) woman who had received it from her ancestors.

This is that story:

> *I was angry. "Why," I asked the Grandmothers, "did you deny your heritage—our heritage? How could you adopt the ways of the white man, the conqueror, and embrace the ways of people who disrespect the Earth Mother? How could you conceal from future generations their own identity and conceal even from your children that you and they were Cherokee? How could you do these things? How could you?" I felt betrayed by my own ancestors.*

> *The smile was gentle and wise, but the voice was firm. It reverberated with strength. Power. "Standing Feather, you have much to learn. You will study the medicine of the Corn Mother and you will understand. We chose our path out of knowledge—the true and lasting knowledge of who and what we are as a people, the teachings of the Great Mystery and the Earth Mother, and the wisdom of the Selu. Do not be quick to judge. You do not know the whole truth, do not understand our purposes."*

> *I trembled, but the fire still burned. I had to know. "How could you?" I saw missed opportunities—traditions forgotten, precious wisdom lost, and a world badly in need of knowledge that was no more—would never be again. Tears stung my eyes.*

Laughter, and gentle chiding—"Standing Feather, you are as a child. Your tears are for nothing, the foolish whining of an infant who only considers herself and lacks the wisdom required for understanding. Stop this nonsense and be about your true mission. You walk your path for a purpose. Do not waste your tears. Our heritage is alive and well. It grows stronger with each sun. Help our people, do not cry for them. Respect our ways, do not see them as diminished or lost. Honor our wisdom. Use your heritage with pride. Everything we had—everything you think we denied—all you believe is lost—is whole and strong, and living in your world. It waits for you now. You only have to claim it."

I saw no way this could be. So much was gone, so much forgotten, so much swept away because it was denied. Lost. Surely they didn't understand.

"But Grandmother, for so many years I did not even know of my heritage. I didn't hear the stories, didn't learn of the healing, didn't know the beauty of the Great Mystery. I admired our people from a distance, not knowing I was one of them. My heart broke for their sorrow and for what was lost . . ."

"Have you learned nothing? You felt a kinship with the people you watched from a distance, even without understanding it. You carry our ways and our wisdom within you. They are as complete as your spirit and as available as your heart, yet you cry for them. You require the most elementary instruction. Put out your hand. Touch what you seek. It is all there, waiting for you. It has always been there."

"But you said you were Black Dutch, born in a foreign land. You denied . . ."

"The most elementary instruction. What hangs on the wall in your home? What rests on the table, on the hearth? What sits beside the door?"

"Grandmother, I don't understand."

"Answer."

"There are pictures of my children and grandchildren, a chain carved from a single length of cedar, ears of dried Indian corn, a painting of the hills and trees in winter, a staff with prayer ties, a raw crystal from the Earth, a length of finger-woven leather strips, a quilt and a rug made by some of you, a vase of pheasant feathers, a wood carving of Chief Dragging Canoe, a hand-woven basket . . ."

"We chose our path deliberately. Times were hard. Our people, our ways, were in danger of annihilation. We were hunted like the deer. There was no place we could go that was safe. Our land and our possessions were stripped from us. Homes burned, people killed. Many died. Our children were taken away to boarding schools and forbidden to speak our language. Sometimes we never saw them again. There were prohibitions against our ceremonies. Our very beliefs were outlawed. The spirit of our people was dying. We had to find a way to preserve these things."

There was a pause and I felt the eyes upon me, burning through to my soul.

"We turned for help to Grandmother Corn, and she taught us how to survive. We studied her teachings. We practiced her ways. One tiny kernel of corn carries everything that is needed to nourish our people physically and spiritually for all time, with enough left over to provide the same for an entire world. Within that one kernel, one seed, there is food, fuel, material to build homes, ceremonies, teaching, nourishment for the spirit, wisdom—the greater part of what is needed for a people to survive.

"The way of the seed is the way Grandmother Corn survives, has survived for thousands, perhaps millions, of seasons. The grain of corn, the single seed, carries the heart and the spirit of the mother. When it is planted in the sweet Earth, it rests, then when the time is right, it comes forth. It grows. First the sprout, then the blade, then

the cornstalk and the ears. It is the Mother reborn, with her heart and spirit intact.

"We knew then that we must do as Grandmother Corn does. We took all that was important to us and drew it deep within our spirit. It could not be seen by the outside world, just as the spirit of Grandmother Corn is not apparent in the seed. What appears to be is not always what is. We kept the seeds hidden and protected, knowing that when the time was right they would come forth and produce fruit. We trusted the ways of the Creator, the Earth Mother, and Grandmother Corn. Our seed, our spirit, would live dormant but intact in future generations. When conditions were right, our people's ways would live again. Nothing would be lost. It was the only way we could survive.

"The white man didn't understand the way of the seed. He didn't know how the Earth Mother can encourage the seed to bring forth the mature plant and the ears of corn. He believed that he could force us to speak his language, wear his clothes, follow his beliefs, and our ways would die. The white man would devour our people, make them part of himself, and we would be no more.

"We allowed him to believe that, and his own belief defeated his purpose. We wore the clothes, spoke the language, and appeared to follow his beliefs. We raised our children in his ways, not telling them of their heritage. But we had placed our spirit and all that was important to us in our seed. Children, grandchildren, and great grandchildren carried it, unknown but safe. The white man could not take it from us.

"Nothing could destroy it. We looked into the swirling mists of the future and we saw our Nation rise again from the many seeds we had planted. We saw the ceremonies and the traditions once again. We heard the stories, found the wisdom passed from generation to generation. We saw our baskets woven by other hands, our clothing *covering other bodies, our songs sung by other voices. But they were we, and we were they. We lived again, and all that was important to us flourished. It is the way of the corn.*

"The white man is not the conqueror. He never was. He was defeated long ago, participated in his own defeat. The white man has always lived in the outside world, always cherished his material things—money, houses, status. That is why his ways can't endure. Those things never mattered to us.

"We long ago learned the lesson of the corn. We carry with us what is important: our spirit. And our spirit will never die, never be diminished. Our blood rushes through your body, our heart beats in your chest, and our thoughts fill your mind. You are our seed. You are Cherokee. Whatever else you are or may be, you are still of our people. You carry our spirit and the hope of our Nation. Honor us.

"Allow us to live again through you. Bring forth our traditions, our stories and ceremonies, our knowledge and beliefs and wisdom. They will serve you well.

"Never forget the teaching of Grandmother Corn. And know that through the centuries, when men and women travel far from Mother Earth, when they do things that you can't even dream of now, they—your children, your grandchildren—will carry with them the seed we planted. And the seed of Grandmother Corn. They will grow corn in many places. And the Cherokee Nation will flourish, will survive to be reborn again and again in the hearts and minds, the spirits, of its children."

When I first read that story of Selu (the Corn Mother), tears rolled down my cheeks and I fell silent. I could feel a collision of feelings, memories, ancestral awakenings, intuitions, and knowings all swirling within me. I felt dizzy and sharply awake at the same time. Most of all, I knew that I had to sit with and wait with what was to come.

I could hear my mother and my great-grandmother, both of a medicine line, saying to me when I was little, "Remember, Elizabeth Anne, it is the unseen that is the most important."

And, I knew that this story was touching knowings and yearnings that I might, someday, be able to articulate. They were in my blood—my very DNA.

The unseen is like this. It is denied by the white world, called superstitious, unreal, imagination, unscientific, and nonexistent. Yet, I could see its reality in my own small world as I was growing up. I saw this truth demonstrated again and again, by my mother and great-grandmother, that the unseen was real and needed to be honored and respected. And, when one knew how to work with it for the good of all creation, the unseen was healing, powerful, and moved toward wholeness.

So I sat with this story for some time, letting it work within me and waited with what was to come.

I knew that the dominant white European culture had worked hard to assimilate us. (This proved to be extremely difficult, even impossible.) For the dominant culture, assimilation meant making us "white." We were to think white, live white, feel white, dress white, believe that white was "reality," and be white. Our minds, thinking, and behavior were relatively easy. And, our beliefs, ancient wisdom, souls, and our beings did not tag along so easily.

Somewhere, deep inside, we have been waiting for . . . something . . .

I slowly came to know that this story of Standing Feather was my story.

I was born at a time (1934) when Native American children were being taken to boarding schools. I recently realized that my entire family on both sides made the painful decision to hide our heritage for my sake. They wanted me to have all the advantages of a white person and not be taken away from them to be brainwashed in a completely white way of being. They knew that living and being, in the long run, would be stronger than superficial teachings—so they waited.

When I was seven, we left the comfort of Cherokee surroundings. My father started working in electronics for the government, and we lived all over the US.

I knew that this "leaving" was especially difficult for my mother. I now realize that to keep the seed alive she did many things that seemed somewhat strange at the time: 1) Wherever we went, she made sure that I knew, honored, and respected the story and history of the Native people of that land. 2) She dragged me through every Indian museum she could find. 3) Our house was filled with photos, woven baskets, crystals, and symbols of our heritage. 4) Most important, she made sure that we returned to the land of our ancestors every year and visited the graves of our ancestors buried in the cemetery adjacent to the first church built at the end of the Trail of Tears of the Cherokee people. She made sure we drank the water of Ballard Springs and, I now realize, insisted that I "be among my people" even if I had no idea that this was what she was doing.

Years later, as a successful, well-educated "white woman," I felt stunned when my old auntie off-handedly said to me, "Oh, by the way, you know you are Cherokee, don't you? Your father was Cherokee."

I felt my mind and body go into an altered state. The only words I have are that I felt the "tumblers of my soul" click into place.

It was as if, at last, my whole life made sense to me. No wonder I felt I had never "belonged." I didn't. I had learned well. I had two doctorates, one earned and the other honorary. I was successful in every aspect valued by the dominant society—money, influence, possessions, and power. Yet what was most important to me had only fallen into place when I heard, "You know you are Cherokee, don't you?" and the tumblers of my soul clicked in.

After this information of my heritage fell into place, I did some research and found that "Black Irish" meant Irish/Indian, and that I had Cherokee blood from both my mother's side and my father's side.

I spent several months being very angry with my family and resentful that they had chosen for us to "pass" because we looked white.

Then, I realized that they had made this terrible sacrifice to protect me and, even later, I realized the wisdom of our ancestors.

They had taught me to *be* Cherokee in every aspect of my living and being and never said what they were teaching me was Cherokee. I now see clearly that they carefully groomed me in the wisdom of my people.

This wisdom did not make my life easy, yet it always made it interesting. I remember when I left the "nest" of my family and went to college. I did not know that I was Native American then and, subliminally, I knew "something" when I called my parents and said, "You have not prepared me for this culture."

They took a lot of heat from me over the years waiting for the right time for me to find out who I really was. I now see that this subterfuge was not easy for any of us. And, I see why it was necessary.

The Native New Zealand people, the Maori, and before them, the Waitaha, and the Mayans talk of a time when the stars are aligned in a certain way and that will be a time for the ancient wisdom to come forth.

All my life, Native people the world over have said that I was one of them. I did not want to be a "wannabe" and always replied, "I know what you mean, but as far as I know, I am Irish and English."

Then, we waited.

We all were waiting for our stars to be aligned to have the knowledge and use it in the right way. The clouds are clearing—not just for me—for many people.

That time seems to be now.

There are many of us. More than any of us know.

Learning the ways of the dominant culture has been relatively easy for us as the Tsa La Gi (Cherokee) demonstrated ages ago. We became so good at learning the white ways and so successful at it in the early years when white people came to live among us that we became a threat. Hence, a Trail of Tears was "needed."

Yet, *why* that culture functions the way it does or why anyone would want to function that way continues to confound us to this day. Again and again, I see people with Native blood appear to be naïve in dealing with the dominant culture when, from my experience, we just continue to be astounded and disbelieving that people would lie or make a sacred agreement and not keep it. How could they not understand that all creation is one and totally interrelated? Can they not see that everything material we have comes from the earth and we must care for and protect that source of goodness for years to come? Our disbelief in anyone's not knowing these truths paralyzes us; putting us into a state of shock and horror.

Indeed, we have never unconsciously considered assimilation even when unaware of the blood of our ancestors coursing through our veins.

What we have known and what I came to know consciously as I sat with the impact of the story of Selu upon me, is that we have not and could not be assimilated. That is why—to this day—Native people are seen to be a threat.

Our ancestors were on to something much bigger and more important than what a materialistic, consumer society could envision.

I came to see that our old ones had "seeded" the blood of this nation for a time when the wisdom of our ancestors held in those seeds would reawaken and come forth.

Many Native elders the world over have said that a time would come when our wisdom would be needed to save the planet.

Most believe that that time is now. It is clear that the Native elders and those who have been raised "Native" cannot do it alone.

They need the support of those whose blood has been "seeded." They/we need all the brilliance we can muster to pull together to save this land and this planet.

It is not possible to solve the problems we face using the thinking, techniques, philosophy, and worldview of the system that created these problems.

"You can't fix the problem with the problem."

We need to return to wholeness and the ability to participate in the process of all creation.

This is not a book to focus on the problems, inadequacies, and malfunctioning of the dominant system. That time is long past.

Those of us who are the "seeded ones" need to learn how to return to be Native in our souls. The teachings, the approaches, techniques, and ways of the dominant culture are powerful and seductive. It is, admittedly, difficult to stand outside that culture, pull its tentacles out of our brains, and begin to see both (and all!) cultures clearly so we can make informed decisions about what is best for all creation.

It is relatively easy to learn how to *act* like a Native person. After several centuries of assimilation, it takes more time and effort to remember how to "be" Native and live out of that beingness.

In this book, I hope to focus on helping those who have Native blood experience what it means to live out of that Nativeness. We do not have to give up anything if it is useful and healing to ourselves, our spirit, and all creation.

We are only returning.

Acting like Native people is easy. Anyone can do it and many do—smudging, picking and carrying sage, doing sweats, even doing ceremonies. *Being* Native is something different altogether.

This book is not about *pretending* to be Native. We have pretended too much already. This book is about being Native from the inside out.

For most of us, this Native state of being will be comforting and a great relief.

This book is not written to incite, upset, or alienate. My hope is that it will be a comforting return to our essence, living out of what makes sense to us at our deepest—our "unseen"—levels of consciousness.

Remember, it is often the unseen, our dreams, our sudden awarenesses, our "whisperings," our intuition that give us our most important knowings. The unseen affects us greatly. As we bring more of our unseen in us into consciousness, we have the opportunity to become more who we are, who we can be, and who we are meant to be.

It is out of our fullness and our wholeness that we can make our best contributions—contributions that can, indeed, heal the planet and all creation.

When I thought of writing this book, one of my working titles was *For Red Eyes Only*. I wanted to offer comfort, healing, and wholeness to those who have been struggling, consciously or unconsciously, with the call of their ancestral blood. Yet, at some level, I believe this is all of us.

We are, after all, created by the same Creator. We are all "Native." For some, it will be a farther reach to return to the teachings than for others, and for all, this returning has meaning.

In sharing what *being* Native means, I will have to call on the teachings of my great-grandmother, my grandparents, my mother, and my father. All, I see now, patiently and skillfully planted "seeds" in me to know another way of being in this world—not just doing—being—that comes from a very different paradigm. There also have been many Native elders who have "taken me on" to help me return to and remember what the seeded DNA in my blood knows. I am sure they will, as always, give me the help I need if I but listen. Frank Fools Crow, the great spiritual leader of the Lakota Sioux, who gave me my name and whose pipe I carry, and my great-grandmother, Mary Elizabeth Reed, never leave my side, and I know that this book is of their choosing—Rolling Thunder, Tsa La Gi; Phil Lane Sr., Yankton Sioux; Jeanette Timentwa, Colville; Rueben Kelly, Koori; Lee Piper, Bill Black, Tsa La Gi; Franklin Kahn, Navajo; Horace Axtell, Nez Perce; Peggy Williams, George Good Striker, Rufus Good Striker, all Blood Blackfeet; have all passed, and their teachings and wisdom always whisper in my ears. Max Thomas, Cherokee; Calvin Williams, Blood Blackfeet; Mary Kahn, Navajo; Andrea Axtell, Nez Perce; all of whom are still with us, plus numerous Native people the world over like Anaru Mapa, Maori; give so freely. Clearly, so many have contributed to my growth and healing that to mention them all would require a book unto itself.

Many of us have tried desperately to fit in. We have tried out ways of behaving and being that have never been right for us. We have become educated in the ideas and ways of the society. We have tried to "pass" and often could get away with it because we do not "look Native." It was also easy to "pass" because many people do not believe that there are any Native Americans left, and if we do exist, they don't want us to be here. We have been silent and invisible—for a reason.

Yet, somewhere, down deep, there is a niggling whisper that sometimes crescendos into a roar that says: SOMETHING IS WRONG!

We are wrong. We are missing our lifeblood and we don't even know it. We have that proverbial itch that won't be scratched and we have scratched ourselves everywhere we could imagine. We know that there is something different, something more, another way, and we don't know where to find it.

Don Coyhis, Mohican, of the White Bison Society, tells this story that was given to him by an elder:

> *The elder tells us of a time long ago when the elders realized that the world was taking a very bad turn for the worst. The Human Race had lost its way, made some very bad decisions, seemed to have forgotten that we all are part of the whole, and was drifting further and further from its spiritual core.*
>
> *So the elders decided to call all the most respected and revered elders together to come up with a plan to save the wisdom, which they saw at risk of being lost and destroyed.*
>
> *One of the elders rose to call the meeting together. His gray hair shone in the firelight and time had etched his face with the wisdom of many winters.*
>
> *"My friends, my brothers and sisters, we have come together to share our wisdom and make some decisions.*
>
> *"I am sure that you have noticed that our world is in pain," he continued.*
>
> *The silver heads nodded in agreement, and a soft murmur of knowing and understanding pulsed through the assembly of gathered elders.*

"As the elders, it is our responsibility to see that the wisdom of our ancestors is not lost and is preserved for all people when they have grown enough to use it wisely."

Again, there was no dissent, and the elders nodded and spoke soft words of agreement to those who sat nearby.

"We need to decide what we must do to keep the wisdom safe so it can come forth when it is needed. It is not safe now because even some of our own people would abuse this wisdom, sell it for money or alcohol, destroy it, not know how to care for it, or not value it for what it is."

Again, nods and murmurs of assent. Some sat silent as tears crept down their cheeks with memories too painful to whisper even to themselves. Then there was silence as the elders sat with this vastly important problem. Each elder went deep inside—as elders tend to do when faced with something so vast and so important. All was quiet as prayers and messages were sent, asking for help and guidance.

After a very long period of silence—which seemed quite short to those gathered there—one of the elders rose to speak. "I have been told that there is a cave deep in the woods which is known to very few people. It is a very deep cave and well hidden. We could wrap all the wisdom in a big bundle with many skins and bury it deep in the cave. It would be safe there."

A murmur sped through the group. Maybe this would work. A few sporadic nods passed between the elders and then, as if by command, silence fell.

"This is a good idea," said another elder, "and very creative. Yet, I fear it would not work."

Several elders looked disappointed.

Then another sighed and said, "Yes, I fear you are right. These people are snoopy. They look everywhere and get into everything. That's what they are like. Eventually they would find it. That won't work."

Sadly, with an air of resignation, all agreed. Then, the group fell silent again.

After an indeterminable passage of time, another rose to speak. "I know of a very deep lake. It is so deep that no one has ever found the bottom. We could wrap the wisdom in something that will keep the water out, put weights on it and hide it at the bottom of that lake."

Again, there were excited nodding heads and murmurs of "good," "It will work," and "What a good idea!" heard in the group. All were relieved to have found such a good idea. Soon their task would be completed. Then, slowly—very slowly—the jubilation subsided and silence engulfed them in the awareness that this would not work either.

Finally one spoke, "This, too, is a very good idea and—they are very inventive—in time they will find the bottom of the lake and when they do, they will find the wisdom bundle, and the wisdom will not be safe."

With great reluctance and sadness, all slowly and painfully had to agree.

It was late and the elders were all getting tired. Yet, they had a grave responsibility, and they all knew that they would do whatever they needed to do to come to the right solution.

All again fell silent. Each in his or her own way was asking the Creator to help them come to the right solution for all the generations that would come. Each knew this was probably the most important task that would ever be asked of them and, with the help of the Creator, they would complete it. Time passed. Some looked like they were dozing, as elders sometimes do. Yet, all knew they were waiting with the right answer.

No one stirred. All was silent.

After more time than any could imagine, the oldest elder, a woman, slowly and painfully rose to her feet. Leaning heavily on her richly carved cane, she began to speak. Although all were very weary, their eyes glistened with attention as her words slowly left her mouth.

"I have prayed and I have listened for the knowing that would come to me for I know this decision is of more importance than any of us can ever possibly imagine."

Although tired, all were alert and listened carefully, for this old woman was known to have kept her relationship with the Creator open and respectful for more winters than many of them had lived. They fixed their eyes on her and leaned in to her.

"I believe that we need to hide the wisdom somewhere where they will never find it until the time is right."

All heads nodded in agreement.

"There is only one place where we can do that," she said with a firm knowing in her voice.

All leaned in farther. A shiver of excitement ran through the group. Their faces were open and expectant as she paused. All sensed that she had discovered the answer that would be the one they needed.

The old elder took a deep breath. She closed her eyes and seemed not to breathe. The suspense was palpable. "We will hide it inside of them," she said. "They will never look there."

A swift, silent pause—no one moved or spoke—then—jubilation.

"Yes!"

"She's right."

"That's the perfect place."

"No safer place."

Everyone was happy, tired, and satisfied.

They had their answer.

And so the wisdom was put inside each person.

To this day, few have looked deep enough to find it.

This book is to assist your looking deep inside yourself to unearth the wisdom that your ancestors buried so carefully in your Native blood.

As is typical in Native writings, much of the teaching will be circular. There will be descriptions of process that will be artificially separated into linear topics and each will enfold and return to the other for the best approximation I can make of the wholeness in linear form.

There are many aspects to every lesson that approaches us, and each of us will be able to hear that lesson with the ears, wisdom, and presence we have at that moment. At another time, the lessons to be learned may sound completely different to us and we will learn at a different level. That is how it should be.

It is only as we learn to *be* Native from our soul out that the wisdom will begin to emerge. Being Native cannot come from our heads.

The Beginning
How we can approach coming into being.

The First Process
The Sacred/Spiritual
Everything is sacred. When we lose track of this truth, we lose ourselves.

The Second Process
Honoring Elders and Children
Our true wealth is in respecting our elders and children.

The Third Process
Participating in the Wholeness
We are a part of a whole.
We are neither better than nor worse than anyone.
We are all equal in the eyes of the Creator and are responsible to participate in helping the whole to be whole.

The Fourth Process
All Is Relationship
Everything is in relationship.
When we see ourselves in relationship with everything—ourselves, others, things, plants, animals, bugs, nature—and take responsibility for our part of those relationships, we act differently.

The Fifth Process
Honor and Respect
Honor and respect are key to all relationships.
Treating everything with honor and respect changes us from the inside out.

The Sixth Process
Nature
We are not above or detached from nature. We are only a part of a participatory nature.

The Seventh Process
Process and Participation
Everything is in process and is a process. We waste our lives when we try to control processes. Our job is to participate in the processes as they are presented to us.

The Eighth Process
Honesty
He or she who lies brings down destruction and disconnection. Honesty is essential for our health.

The Ninth Process
The Process of Co-Creating
As we participate we become co-creators with all that is around us.

The Tenth Process
Valuing Differences
Differences present a possibility for growth and learning. Differences are not, as seen in the dominant culture, a threat.

The Eleventh Process
Being of Service
We are here to learn, heal, and be of service. Being of service is a major way we learn and heal.

The Twelfth Process
Living in Our Bodies and Taking Care of Them
The care of and living in our bodies.

The Thirteenth Process
Listening and Humor
No one listens like an Indian.

The Fourteenth Process
Living in Context—Don't waste, don't abuse
Living in context is a way of affirming wholeness and all interrelatedness.

The Fifteenth Process
Science
The world of the Native person is expansive and emerges from wholeness.

The Sixteenth Process
Thinking
The process of thinking for the Native person requires the participation of the whole being interactive with our context.

The Seventeenth Process
Patience
Patience is trusting the process of God, the Creator, a Higher Power, whatever you call it.

The Eighteenth Process
Humility
Our ancestors practiced a form of humility that is peculiar to a Native worldview.

The Nineteenth Process
Prayer
All life, all action, all being—each of these is an act of prayer.

The Twentieth Process
The Unseen
Much of the world of our ancestors was informed by process of the unseen. Suspicion and denial of the unseen have not erased the existence of the unseen; we have access to a clear awareness of the unseen and an informed interaction with it.

The Twenty-First Process
Living in Balance
We are here to maintain and create balance. It is as it should be that we move away from balance, for we need to learn. Yet, we need to focus our energy on returning to balance or moving to a new balance.

In Summary
Creating a Wholeness of Being
As we respond to the call of our ancestral blood, we become living, knowing, beings of action.

Each section is short. Hopefully, in each one we will move from information, to understanding, to feeling, to living out of what we have learned. Each will include teaching stories and ways to move into being.

There will be help to move from "learning about," to emulating, to being.

Being Native is a state of mind, body, soul, belief, and worldview.

When the Native wisdom of our ancestors is involved in all we think, feel, know, and do, we have choices about how we will *be* that wisdom.

The Beginning

WRITTEN FORM IS NOT THE WAY most of our elders chose to teach. Our people respect writing as a way of recording and communicating. The Cherokee had a written language long before other peoples came to this land.

Yet the chosen form of teaching that our ancestors used was a slow, gentle form of situational, participatory teaching that involved listening, observation, example, storytelling, and developing the skill of noticing.

Teaching was constant. It began in the womb and was lifelong, as the person was ready for the next level of understanding. It was never static or linear. Learning was assumed to be as essential as breathing and continued until death. I have heard some elders say that, in the old days, by the time a child was six or eight they had acquired the equivalent of a college degree in science, math, language, and sociology in the understanding of their world.

Our ancestors had time to teach in this practical, participatory way because they had everyone doing the teaching (It Takes a Village to Raise a Child!), and their lives were not so controlled by materialism.

One old Australian Aboriginal elder told me that they "lived the life of an English country gentleman before the white people came." He said that little of their time was spent in "work" as their land was generous and the food and all they needed was all around them. This lack of focus on working to attain material things left them plenty of time for teaching the children song, dance, and spiritual growth, which he saw are not so easy to teach in the current approach of the society.

Many who will read this book will not have the advantage that I now see I had in the way I was taught and the learning opportunities I had. I was surrounded by people who knew the old ways even though they never really identified them as such.

I had parents, grandparents, a great-grandmother, uncles, and a whole community who participated in the process of my on-the-spot learning. I was so fortunate.

I remember a constant flow of:

"Look here, Elizabeth Anne, let's see how this machine works." Or:

"Watch the bug. See how it gathers the manure and makes it into a ball larger than the bug is, yet can easily roll it to a safe place. The bug puts its eggs inside the manure ball where they will be safe and have something to eat until they are ready to face the world. Isn't that amazing? The Creator has created so many ingenious ways to be in this world. That bug is called a dung beetle." Or:

"Of course you can help me cook. Pull that chair up to the counter so you can reach and we will make Grandma's famous pecan pie together."

Over seventy years later, I still remember the recipe and how she put it together, and now I am "famous" for my pecan pie.

I share all this about learning because one of my main concerns about writing this book is that a book, by default, is left-brain learning. A book involves more thinking than participation and doing. It involves more information than experiencing. It pulls us into a way of learning that is more Western European than Native American. Reading is a more informational than participatory example. I can talk about how you can begin to be more Native in your being and it is much more difficult to teach this way than by doing things together.

For example, with the group of people I invited to my home to help me prepare my Indian room and learn more about their possible "Nativeness," most mentioned that their most significant "learnings" about honoring all creation came from the way I treated the antique quilts as we slowly sorted them. Each quilt, the maker, and the materials were touched, discussed, and valued as we took the time each deserved to complete the task. They also noticed that I brought the same respect to garbage and the recycling that I brought to the quilts. And, as we worked together they learned something about honoring all creation in all that we do— something they had not learned as they seized a task and pushed through with the focus on getting it done.

According to most, these participatory experiences were much more important to their learning about *being* Native than anything I said.

Yet, I still feel that there are many who *need* a book like this, whose souls hunger for a book like this, and whose "awakening" to their Native wisdom is essential for the planet at this time.

So, as Martin Luther said, "Sin bravely so that grace will abound." I will sin bravely in sharing this wisdom and hope it will, as my elders have assured me, feed and water the seeds that have been planted in each of us to bring forth the wisdom that is so needed on the planet at this time.

With the help of my ancestors, my elders, my teachers, and the Great Spirit, I trust that I will find a way with the words to say and do what needs to be done. I am very clear that I cannot impart this teaching by myself.

Frank Fools Crow, the great Lakota Sioux spiritual leader, used to say that in and of himself he was nothing. He said that in all of the thousands of healings and miracles that he performed, he did none of them. He was a hollow bone. It was the Great Spirit working through him that did the healings and miracles.

I am so aware of the truth in that statement. I know I am at my best when I get out of the way and allow the wisdom and the power of the Creator to work through me. I have tried to live my life in this way and do whatever the Great Spirit asks of me to the best of my ability.

I hope to be able to be the hollow bone through which this book comes to share these important teachings. I know that I will not be perfect in doing this. No human is perfect and I certainly am no exception. I will need the help of my ancestors, my elders, and my teachers who have gone before me to do this task. I pray to be open to the guidance that is there for me.

I pray only to make myself available to write a book to awaken this wisdom within those who are ready for it. This wisdom is, after all, like in Selu, the kernel of corn, already there. It only needs to be awakened and nurtured.

Now, we have begun.

Let's move on to the teachings about being Native.

The First Process
The Sacred/Spiritual

EVERYTHING IS SACRED.

When we lose touch with this truth, we lose ourselves.

Sacredness/spirituality cannot be relegated to a certain time and a certain place. Spirituality cannot be separated into categories, hierarchies, persons, or places. All is sacred.

Most Native languages the world over do not have a word for spiritual—because the spiritual/sacred is everywhere, everything.

This separation of ourselves, who we are, and what we do, from the sacred is one of the confusions that our ancestors felt with the "newcomers." How could they not know that hunting was sacred? How could they not know that planting was sacred? Did they not see the miracle, the infinite miracle, in the large plant that came from the tiny seed?

The newcomers seemed to think that if their minds understood "how" the plant came forth, this eliminated the miracle and the mystery. How confusing! The "understanding" only made the miracle more miraculous because, if we are honest, we can see that our science can only take us so far in our understanding and then the miracle has to take over. The enchantment returns.

We can understand the molecules in a piece of wood. Yet how do these molecules come together to make the wood?

It has been said that we are not human beings trying to be spiritual, we are spiritual beings trying to learn how to be human.

Our ancestors knew this truth. Everything around us is an affirmation of the sacred. The sun rising, the day ending, a time of rest. The seasons when all of nature rests, gathers strength, and springs forth again. Who cannot see that this process of being born, living, dying, and again coming forth is sacred?

When we live according to the wisdom of our ancestors, everything is sacred.

Eating, preparing the food, making love, going to the bathroom—all are sacred acts. In each we participate in a process that is much larger than any of us, and that connection is sacred.

Sacredness cannot and should never be set apart. The activity and the process are one and are infinitely connected.

A group of us have had the honor of putting our money into and taking care of a beautiful old place in Montana called Boulder Hot Springs. There are few who grew up in Montana who do not have some connection to Boulder Hot Springs. The old building sits nestled into the hillside looking over the Little Boulder and Boulder Rivers and the Boulder Valley rimmed by mountains on all sides except toward the south where the valley continues down to its south-rimming mountains. Its forty or so hot springs pour out of the ground, sending their mineral-laden water to enrich the rivers. The old building is California Mission and a bit like something out of a Stephen King movie.

Yet the history of this place goes back long before the buildings.

The first people of that place knew that this land was especially sacred and a gift from the Creator because the hot mineral waters were so healing. In fact, even tribes who had historical hostilities would not fight there because it was such a sacred place. Tribes came together to trade, have ceremonies, and heal. They called this valley Peace Valley.

I knew an elder from the Colville Reservation who went there to soak and trade as a child. Before her death in her late nineties, she shared many teachings with us about the sacredness of the water, how we should treat the water and how we could ask it for help. I was grateful to have participated in many ceremonies with her in the hot plunges and natural steam rooms. We sang "her song," moved in the four directions in the water, pausing to say prayers in every direction. We brought sacred cedar boughs into the steam and sprinkled the sacred waters in prayer.

She always admonished us to remember to pray to the water and thank it for all its sacred gifts. Most people just come in and soak and take. She taught us to respect and maintain the sacred balance.

When we start treating every aspect of our lives—from the pen that is writing this book, to the paper it is written on, to the computer that types the manuscript, to the publisher who prints it, to the printing of the book, to the artist who designs the cover, to the eyes that read it as sacred, we begin to experience how our lives might change if we approached everything as sacred. Our illusion of control, our self-centeredness, our arrogance—might all dissolve before our very eyes.

Participating in the Process of the Sacred

Practicing the Sacred

When you take your morning shower or go to the waters at sunrise as every good Cherokee would do, treat the waters as sacred. Also, as well, treat your body and the area where you bathe in a sacred way.

Daily, recognize and give thanks for the waters. Approach the clothes you wear as sacred. For those who cook, approach the preparation of the food as a sacred act. When you get caught up in approaching the food preparation as a task to be completed—stop—regroup—and return to the awareness of the sacredness of the food and the process of what you are doing with it.

Every day expand your awareness of the sacred—your car—your home—a tree—relationships . . .

How do you feel different?

Allow the whisperings of your ancestors to encourage you in your growing wisdom of the sacredness of all creation.

Don't just think about all being sacred.

Behave out of this awareness.

Show care and gratitude for all that is around you. Take nothing for granted. Always see the beauty—all beauty.

The Second Process

Honoring Elders and Children

OUR ELDERS CONNECT US with the ancient accumulated wisdom of the past. Our children are our cultural savings account for the future in which we can invest the wisdom of our ancestors (not our biases, prejudices, even beliefs). We can pass on what wisdom we have gathered by participating in the process of life.

Our elders offer us something that is not accessible anywhere else. They knew someone, who knew someone, who knew someone who lived in a different time in a different way. They help us to begin to realize the unreality of our current culture and the biases of the worldview that generated a particular culture. Elders help us to transcend time and space and return to our deeper *knowings*.

I have never seen any one thing be as effective in changing a person or a group as plunging into the process of respecting our elders.

No matter who your elders are, or what they have done, they deserve some respect for passing on the seed of life, having learned some things in the passage of years that you just are not privy to yet, and having information and experiences that are no longer available. The process of honoring our elders forges deep shifts in our well-constructed (and often necessary—we believe) suits of armor that we have developed to survive in the world in which we live.

Almost twenty years ago, I had invited an international group of people with whom I had been working to a Gathering of Native elders from all over the world. We all were excited about this coming together and awaited it with great anticipation. The first day of the Gathering, I was beyond appalled with the behavior of many people toward the elders. They got in front of them as we lined up to eat. They rushed ahead of them and bumped them when passing. They rushed into the meeting room and put their belongings on the seats to reserve the best seats in the meeting room. I was horrified and embarrassed. I felt like a parent who had raised some very unruly children.

I called a meeting of the people who behaved so badly, and I was livid. I mercilessly reamed them out and was almost blind with anger and humiliation (nobody said I was perfect—least of all me). When I was able to see beyond my rage, I noticed that many were weeping and others had tears rolling down their faces. I had a fleeting thought of "serves them right" and then, in true Native fashion, compassion set in.

"What's going on?" I asked.

"We don't know how to treat elders!" they wailed. "No one ever taught us."

I was incredulous. "No one ever taught you?" I asked in disbelief.

"No one," they said, and the tears flowed.

Training in how to treat elders started in the womb with me. I could not believe that a group of people existed who did not know how to treat elders. It is the basis (or at least one of them) of Native culture. Thus began a training of almost twenty years of helping this group know how to relate to and honor elders . . . all elders.

It has not been a linear learning. There have been slips, excuses of, "My elders were Nazis, how could I honor them?" There have been relapses and struggles. Old habits die hard. And, just this one teaching has brought more changes in the group and the individuals than anyone could have imagined.

People feel better about themselves when they honor elders. When elders are honored, they are happier and share their wisdom more easily.

All are less self-centered.

There is less ageism when being an elder has status.

People are excited to become elders.

People have something to look forward to as they age.

There is more balance in the groups.

Generally people are happier.

Service makes sense.

I have learned a great deal from my reaction of anger and embarrassment. Over the years, I have discovered that many of the ways of being that I learned growing up Native were not shared by all people. When this difference appears, I am shocked, disbelieving, and angry. When people, especially of the dominant culture, behave in a way that is shocking to me, I find myself incredulous. Surely they know better. I assume we all have had the same teaching about the "right" way to be in this world, and we haven't.

This is a lesson I have to keep learning over and over again.

When I shared this story with some of my Hawaiian *ohana* (family), they, too, were shocked and angry when I described the treatment of the elders. Then, when I shared the story of their tears and the pain they felt that no one had taught them how to be with elders, my Hawaiian family burst into tears.

"We can't believe it!" they said. "We always thought that white people knew how to behave and just didn't do it.

"We need to pray for them," they said—a much more compassionate response than mine.

Learning how to treat and relate to elders is like the kingpin in a row of dominos. So many things fall into place as we respect and honor elders.

So, then, how do we treat elders with respect?

In many Native traditions one always comes with an appropriate gift when coming to an elder. Often this is tobacco. The gift needs to be a humble gift and is not about the giver. It is not given to impress the elder. It is not given to prove how savvy one is. It is not given to manipulate or control the elder in any way. It is, pure and simple, to honor who and what the elder is, whatever that means. The gift is not to call attention to ourselves. It is given to honor the elder.

If people want to give special gifts to the elder, it is better to combine them with gifts from others anonymously, so as not to call attention to themselves.

Elders are people. We need to approach them with the love and respect we give to people we love. Elders (true elders) do not like to be fawned over any more than they like to be ignored.

Never be obsequious with an elder. Do not interrupt an elder.

Always listen to what an elder is saying with respect and patience. You never know when you will hear exactly what you need to hear from an elder. They have a sixth sense.

Always be present to an elder and try to anticipate their needs.

Never argue with an elder. You don't have to agree with an elder. You do need to hear them out and later check out what fits for you.

Never walk away when an elder is talking. Hear them out. Never use elders for your own aggrandizement.

Be ready to assist and serve in whatever way you can.

Elders can spot phoniness and cons a mile away. They may not say anything, and they know.

Never assume you know what an elder wants/needs and act on it without checking with the elder.

Never, never push your assumptions and agendas on an elder.

For elders who have grown up in a Native way, it is often shocking the way they are treated by younger people, and they withdraw behind a shield to protect themselves from the shock.

Never organize others to do what you think an elder wants. Let the elder take the lead.

Be present in a state of open anticipation.

Give elders all the good clean love you can. They can take it in like sponges. Always be respectful.

Many of the ways to treat elders above also relate to children.

Children are sacred human beings and should always be treated as such. Children do not exist to validate you and your beliefs or choices.

It is always our responsibility to treat children with loving care.

We need to see that children learn as much as they can about a wide variety of information about everything, including other beliefs and ways so that they can make their own choices.

We need to be able to help children become comfortable in their own selves and in their bodies.

Children should know that they are loved.

We need to help children know that they are a part of and not above nature. Then they will be more secure. Rugged individualism, ironically, does not breed security.

Mistakes are one of our best forms of learning. We need to show our children by example that we accept and honor our mistakes as a very good vehicle for learning.

When I was a child, we played math and grammar games at the dinner table. How we all laughed when I caught my parents in a mistake! How we all laughed when I was caught in a mistake! We were all learning.

It is our responsibility to help our children learn how to honor themselves, others, and all creation.

We need to nourish a lifelong curiosity in children.

We need to help our children learn to be hollow bones in thought, deed, and act. Children learn from us the beauty of service and honoring elders.

The teaching of children needs to be patient and gentle.

The more they know about their world, the more secure they will be in their world. We need to model respecting our bodies, minds, and souls so our children have a touchstone in the future.

Respect is taught by being respected.

When I was five years old, our family explored my father's taking a leave of absence from his work, our leaving the area that was "home," where we were surrounded by family and friends who lived out of a Native paradigm, and going to California to mine gold.

At five, I was given an equal voice in that discussion and decision-making.

"What do you think, Elizabeth Anne?" was an oft-uttered question.

I learned that I was of value and that I was responsible for my decision. Just being told that I was of value and was responsible for my decisions would not have conveyed the same message.

Children and elders are our treasures. When we respect and honor them, we honor ourselves.

Participating in the Process of Honoring our Elders and Children

If you don't have elders and children in your life, what's wrong with you?

Just being in the presence of elders and children stretches us and contributes to our growth.

I have found that I always learn something when I am with an elder. For the purpose of learning how to treat an elder, anyone who is older than you are is an elder to you and should be treated as such.

Make an effort to season your life with elders and children and do more listening than talking.

Let their interests guide the activities that are chosen.

Notice how often you want others to recognize how much you know.

Check to see if your "helpfulness" is more about you than it is about the person you are "helping."

We live in a very self-centered society, and we get a great deal of support to be self-centered and believe that our world circles around ourselves and what we want/need.

Being with elders and children is very good humility training. It is not so easy to give up our agendas, timetables, and flow charts.

Elders and children are often experts at living and participating in the process of their lives.

What can you learn from them?

How difficult is it for you to slow down to another's pace?

Our ancestors knew how to live with all life and creation. How can learning to know our elders feed into that process of knowing?

Elders and children are great for patience and humility training.

The Third Process

Participating in the Wholeness

PERSONS WHO HAVE GROWN UP in a Native paradigm simply cannot understand how anyone could not know the oneness and wholeness of all things.

We are a part of a whole. We ultimately are not better than or worse than anyone or anything. We are all one. We may do bad things. They may do bad things. And, ultimately, we are equal in the eyes of the Creator and as part of the whole.

Since we are all equal in the eyes of the Creator, we therefore are responsible to participate in helping the whole be whole.

Western science is reductionistic and has trained our minds to think that the only way we can understand (i.e., measure, predict, and control) is to reduce everything to its most elemental level and make it static (kill its process) so we can measure, predict, and control. In this process, which is believed to be the only approach to truth, we have lost our awareness of the oneness of all creation and its complete interrelatedness. Then an oil spill comes along to remind us that this kind of thinking is folly.

Even the religions that prefer to believe in one God refuse to acknowledge the oneness of all creation and instead promote racism, righteousness, and feelings of superiority.

Native teachings share none of this folly. To deny the oneness of all creation is to deny the reality of creation.

Virginia Satir, the person who pioneered family therapy, used to use an exercise to demonstrate that the family was like a mobile and functioned as a whole. She would loosely tie everyone together with a continuous rope that ended up where it started. Then, she would ask everyone to start to move around. Very quickly it became clear that if one person tried to act independently all were affected. If one chose to bolt, another was strangled. In order for no one to be injured or killed, they all had to work together to find what worked best for the whole. They were all inextricably bound together.

And so it is with all creation. I am my brother's keeper, and my sister's, and the keeper of people I do not even know on the other side of the planet.

We are slowly beginning to see that we are a very small planet in a very big universe and everything that happens on this planet happens to us all.

Yet, the implications of wholeness and oneness go far beyond some vague awareness that what one does affects The All.

To understand what wholeness and oneness mean to Native people is to embrace what it means to move toward wholeness in all that we are and do, and to understand that all of creation moves toward wholeness.

For example, as human beings, part of our reality is that we experience trauma, make serious mistakes, and, in general, experience life in a way that is fragmenting. As I said, this fragmentation has been encouraged, even demanded, by the dominant culture. Yet, there is something inside of us that pushes us toward wholeness and oneness and encourages us to become whole.

As a psychotherapist (as I then called myself), I worked with people who had experienced such sexual, physical, emotional, and even cult trauma that it was difficult to believe that they could ever again experience wholeness in themselves.

Yet, when they were willing to face their inner process, be honest with themselves and others, and do their work, I could see that they were moving toward greater and greater wholeness.

If I stand back, I can also see that the planet is moving toward greater and greater wholeness, although the path may seem quite zigzagged.

Our ancestors knew about wholeness and the oneness of all creation.

Look at the medicine wheel where the four colors of nations are represented.

I will never forget my first Sundance when I tearfully realized that for hundreds of years our red brothers and sisters had been praying for *all* their relations—the red, the yellow, the black, and the white relations.

"How did they know to do this?" I asked myself. "How did they know that we are all one?"

I am humbled that my ancestors were so brilliant and advanced in their knowledge and their spirituality. Clearly they had tapped into vast stores of wisdom that the dominant culture is only now beginning to become aware of. The science and technology of our Native ancestors' world was so sophisticated. It is very shortsighted to see it as primitive.

Is there any among us who truly believes that the Arabs were created by a different God?

Native people have long said that there is one God and many paths to that God. None of us has all the truth. If we truly respect one another, we can put our truths together to form a larger truth approximating a greater and greater whole. This is what our old ones have told us. How brilliant is that?

It makes such complete sense that if there is one Creator, we are all a part of that creation. How can the Iraqi, the Afghani, the African not be my brothers and sisters? It makes no sense. Humans have created racism, not the Creator. The Creator created one glorious creation.

If we think we are better than or worse than anyone, we are insulting the God of all creation. A time is quickly coming when the only way we can save this beautiful planet is to realize that we all are one, and when a species disappears, a part of each of us dies.

Humans are not the epitome of creation; we are a part of the greater whole. Who is to say that we are more important than the majestic redwood or the mighty whale? Our ancestors have planted the wisdom of the oneness within each of us.

All we have to do is let this wisdom move toward wholeness and stop fragmenting our world.

Our ancestors never addressed the problem of fragmentation because our oneness and interconnectedness was so obvious to them that they could not even conceive that anyone would not know this wholeness from the very core of his or her being.

So much of our current science points in this direction—the repetitions in all the phylum Chordata—the genome project—the basic building blocks of all matter. Yet, we hold on to our separateness, our disconnectedness, and our illusions of a private life.

Participating in the Process of Moving Toward Wholeness

How many of us have visited a foreign country and initially been acutely aware of the differences in appearance, skin color, clothing, languages, customs, and beliefs? Then, when we came to know a few individuals, we were astounded with our similarities. After all, our blood, whatever nation it represents, is the same color.

Just take some time to get to know a tree. Are you really more important than that tree? That tree can live without you. Are you able to live
without it?

Being aware of being a part of a greater whole is such a comfort and
gives one a feeling of security. When we know we are a part of a wholeness that is greater than ourselves, and/or we accept the responsibility for
being a part of that wholeness and participating in it, our lives change.

Franklin Kahn, a Navajo elder, once said to me, "I don't care how a
person prays. What is important to me is *that* he prays. Then he is always
welcome to stand beside me."

Franklin was a man of the Arizona desert and mountains. His bones rest
there now. When looking at him, one could see the desert in him and him
in the desert. He was one with his land, and he was one with all lands and
all people. Such was his intimate knowing of the oneness of all creation.

Participating in the Process of Wholeness

Take a look at the ways you separate yourself from your oneness with
The All that is. Do you hold on to prejudices, resentments, or outgrown
beliefs of your family or society?

What is keeping you from your awareness of the oneness and wholeness
of all creation? Work on it! Leave your comfort zone. Move in to that
which seems unknown.

Begin to offer yourself the comfort of participation in the process of
oneness. Don't *think* about it. Do it!

In Western culture it is easy to say the words, "I believe in one God, the
Creator of heaven and earth," and not act out of this belief.

In Native culture, the words are not that important; *acting* out of the
knowing of oneness is what counts.

The Fourth Process

All Is Relationship

BLACK ELK SAID, "The center of the universe is everywhere." In the Native perspective and in the broadest sense of relationships, relationships are everything. Relationships are, indeed, everywhere. The Native world is composed of a changing infinite number of throbbing, pulsating, modifying energies—all of which are connected—all of which are connected and interdependent, yet unique.

As I write this, the nesting sandhill cranes are calling in the meadows. Are they helping me put these words down on paper? The answer is, of course, *yes!* Nature will always help us when we are open.

I find that this *sense* of relationships as known and experienced by the person raised in a Native way is probably one of the most difficult processes I have attempted to express in English in all my years of trying.

I find it similar to the oft-quoted definition of pornography, "It is difficult to define and I know it when I see it."

In my experience of knowing the fullness of relationships being the center of the universe and being everywhere in everything, there came a time when I "knew" it and I could see it.

This time came when I was writing my second book, *Women's Reality: An Emerging Female System in a White Male Society.* In that book, I described three systems I had observed: 1) The White Male System (WMS), in which the definitions, power, and influence are created and held by white males; 2) The Reactive Female System (RFS), which is a reactive system created by women (and minorities) to relate to and survive in the WMS; and 3) The Emerging Female System (EFS), which, stimulated by the feminist movement, was a system out of another paradigm, which was unconsciously known by women and which had been suppressed by them in order to "fit in" to the dominant system. Later, after working with addicts in recovery and writing about addiction (*When Society Becomes an Addict*), I moved on to see that the WMS was really an addictive system. The characteristics and processes of the dominant system fit perfectly with the characteristics and processes of the alcoholic. The RFS enabled and supported the addictive system and was thus a codependent system. The EFS shared many characteristics of the person in recovery who, in order to take recovery as seriously as it needed to be taken, had to be willing to make a complete paradigm shift, and that system has many characteristics similar to a Native system.

In the last few years I have been focusing on recovering the teachings of my elders and my ancestors. I have seen that many of the elements in what I called the Emerging Female System are also elements of my Native heritage that have been hidden and suppressed in order to survive until the time was right. These are the circles of all our lives. These circles and connections emerge when we recognize the wisdom of what our elders have taught us—life and nature are a series of circles.

In *Women's Reality*, I envisioned a sphere with layers encircling them. In the WMS, the center of the universe was the self and the work—whatever else was in a person's life revolved around the self and the work/money. Relationships, spirituality, whatever—all revolved around and through the self and the work and was defined by the self and the work. This system is built on a self-centered/materialistic universe and the center is not everywhere.

In the EFS and the Native system the center of the universe is everywhere in motion—swirling processes—and these processes are a combination of (in static words) spirituality, relationships, processes, and participation. Everything in our lives, everything that exists, is informed by our spirituality, relationships (in the broadest sense), process, and participation. This combination is the center of our universe, and it is everywhere.

When I say that our relationships are part of the processes of the center of our universe, I do not mean relationships in general like spouses, children, family, and friends. These are not and should not be the center of our universe. It is unhealthy if they are.

In order for a Native person to be balanced and live out of our spirituality, our primary relationship needs to be with our Creator/spirituality/Great Spirit/God. Other relationships are important as are all relationships, and we need to honor and respect them. Yet, we can only live a life of serenity, humility, and service when our primary relationship is with our Creator. Life is much easier when we live that way. We simply are not fighting and struggling with so many of the issues we fight and struggle with in this society when our relationship with our Creator/spirituality is our primary relationship.

I have found that many people can have the concept of having their primary relationship be with their Creator and for people raised in the dominant culture the actual living of this concept is nigh to impossible.

I knew a Native elder whom I loved very much and with whom I had a close relationship. She had devoted most of her life to working with and helping her people and was very knowledgeable in the ways of her tribe. She taught me much in many ways. And, as with the teachings of so many of our most important teachers, the learnings did not always come in a positive or gentle way.

Over the years in working with her, I observed that she seemed to have a blind spot with respect to her family. I knew that there were some difficult dynamics in her family and all was not easy, although she wanted it to be. I saw her tolerate and defend rude and obnoxious behavior in her grandson—behaviors she would never tolerate in other children. I observed that she treated her family very differently than she treated others and always defended it with, "My family comes first no matter what!" This putting our family first is a highly valued virtue in the dominant culture and does not operate the same way in a Native culture. Our families are important to us *and* our relationship with our Creator *has* to be primary for us to walk our path well.

On a gut level I never completely heard this "putting the family first" as a virtue. So, I sat with this for many years—uneasy, a bit confused, and respectful of the honor she so rightly deserved knowing there was something here for me to learn.

At one point she asked if we would arrange airline tickets for her to take her daughter to Branson, Missouri, where her daughter always wanted to go. Her daughter had a serious, progressive disease, and for her mother, this trip was important for her to do.

We had supported her financially in many ways and if she had asked us to pay for the tickets, we probably would have done so. Yet we were feeling that we had done more than enough, were a bit short on money, and were glad she said she would pay for them—it would bring our relationship back in balance! So, we carefully made clear that we would do the work to get the best possible airline tickets, which we did, and she would reimburse us right away. This would maintain a balance in our relationship.

We arranged for and bought the tickets and sent them to her. She and her daughter went to Branson and told us about the wonderful time they had and—no payment. We, respectfully, waited for almost six months. No payment.

We then reminded her of the tickets and the trip to Branson and her agreement to pay us what was a substantial amount.

Her response was, "Oh, yes! Something came up, and I used the money for my family. My family comes first. I'm not going to pay you!"

I felt crushed . . . not about the money, which was difficult. I was crushed that someone I loved and admired was willing to unbalance our relationship and, more important, jeopardize her relationship with her Creator by denying that her relationship with the Creator was her primary relationship and acting accordingly.

I stopped to see how I have jeopardized my relationship with the Great Spirit in the service of a partnership or my children and how I have suffered as a result.

I have seen greatly gifted medicine people get "off track" because of a romantic or sexual relationship and their ability to "be a hollow bone for the Creator" was jeopardized or broken for a while, and their "medicine" suffered. We are all human. We will make mistakes. We need to learn from our mistakes. Often, we don't like the people who see our mistakes.

She taught me, without a doubt, what I had learned from my great-grandmother, that my primary relationship with the Creator is not to be tampered with in any way.

I know that it is difficult to try to deal with and comprehend on so many levels (a bad word) and processes (a better word yet difficult for non-Natives and those raised in a non-Native way) and, yet, that is part of what we are trying to learn in this book. Clearly, a learning so complex, profound, and sophisticated is much better absorbed in person, over time, and with a lot of individual attention, and we will struggle on. Native learning is process, circular, and multidimensional. It is very difficult for linearly trained minds. Yet, we persevere.

When we talk of relationships being truly the center of the universe, we mean that we recognize that every aspect of the universe is interrelated and is in relationship and must relate to and be related through relationships. Nothing is truly static in this kind of a universe. We will never get our relationships—or our lives—perfectly the way we want them. We will never get our homes the way we want them and then walk away knowing they will stay that way. Our homes demand that we be in a relationship with them—a dynamic relationship. The same is true of our cars. We need to establish good relationships with our cars.

I had a 1967 Volkswagen Bug with whom I had a great relationship, established over time. That car taught me to listen to everything it told me. If I didn't, I always got in trouble. Sometimes it spoke to me through sounds—something not sounding right, clicking, squealing, or thumping. Sometimes it spoke to me through smells—something's burning, it doesn't smell right, my nose is hurting. Sometimes it spoke to me through the unseen—intuition—and, because we had a relationship, we had an ongoing dialogue. In the last few years I had that car, if it ever got in trouble it was always in front of a mechanic or a gas station, and I traveled vast, vacant stretches of the West in that car. My VW Bug and I had a good relationship, and I sold it to someone I knew would appreciate it and would take care of it. The money was much less important than knowing it had a good home. We respected each other.

Because I know that I am in relationship with all creation, I live out of knowing that I am related to The All. I am family with all creation.

All humans are my family. When I meet a new person, I assume they are family and I treat them as such. I do not find this difficult because it comes out of my knowing that all is in relationship. I may, after some exploration (and it usually takes me quite a bit of experiencing) decide that this is a "family member" I don't want or need to see often, and that person remains family and I am still available to that family connection. I also feel this relationship with the earth, trees, plants, animals—The All.

There were times when my children were little that I could see that my strong knowing that all are family created pain for us. And we had to deal with that pain. I always treated my children's friends as family and supported them as family.

My son had a very good friend whose family had some problems, and often his good friend came to stay with us for a while. We fed him, loved him, helped him with his homework, and he was "family" to us. For us, this was what our ancestral blood demanded of us, and it was the right thing to do. Over the years, our household was filled with many kids who needed an extra family. It was what we did. It was what my family had done when I was growing up. All were family. It was "normal," it was "how things were done."

Sometimes, it was not always easy for my children when they had to share our resources, love, time, and energy with others, and they rarely complained.

What gave me a great deal of pain over the years was that my children did not get the same treatment from other families. The balance was not kept. The infinity signs were not fed. The "oneness" was not acknowledged.

I have come to know that the pain and confusion I was feeling must be somewhat akin to what my ancestors felt when the "newcomers" first arrived, with their European value system. There is a strange comfort in that knowing.

I also take comfort in knowing that even though my children were not "taken in as family members" by others, it still was the "right" thing for us to do, and living our teachings kept our relationship with the Creator alive and in balance.

I have met many people who speak of "all my relations," and do not demonstrate this way of being in their everyday lives. For Native people— our elders—this "all of my relations" were not just words. It was a way of being in the world.

There are many aspects of good relationships that apply to every relationship, whether it is our relationship with God, or our relationship with a spouse or friend, or our relationship with the larger universe.

We need to be gentle with our relationships. Gentleness is in short supply in such a competitive system. Yet, gentleness is something that our ancestors and elders knew well. I remember years and years ago someone commented that I walked through the woods with great gentleness. Of course I did, I was walking with the Creator among my relations. We may not get a lot of support for gentleness in today's world. It may even be seen as a weakness, yet, to enhance and preserve our relationships, we need to learn gentleness with all our relations.

We need to be respectful with our relationships. Respect also seems to be not so popular in our current world and society and yet respect is necessary in good relationships. By respect, I do not mean being obsequious, fawning, passive, or codependent.

By respect, I mean a person who respects her- or himself in an equal manner offering that same valuing to another, others, or all relations. Only when we truly know that we are equal sharers in a spiritual creation can we have respect for ourselves and others. True respect is possible when we know that all are created equal in the eyes of God and all are valued, necessary parts of the whole. When I come to believe that I am better than or less than, I cannot show respect. I am being self-centered.

Many years ago Frank Fools Crow (Eagle Bear) gave me my name and a pipe to carry. I was totally and completely overwhelmed. I had to write down the name in Lakota and English so as not to forget it as I felt in a complete altered state during and after the ceremony. I was overwhelmed with the name and the honor and responsibility of being a pipe carrier. I felt that I was not good enough and held on to that illusion for many years. I sought advice and help from many of my Native friends and elders and nothing seemed right.

One day, I was talking with one of my friends from the Fort Belknap Reservation, Lenore Stiffarm. She listened to me and my, I now see, whining and began to look quite angry.

"How dare you insult that old man!" she said.

I burst into tears.

"I would never insult Fools Crow. I love him!" I blithered back.

"Then why do you not accept his decision to give you the name he gave you and take the honor and responsibility to carry that pipe for him?" she hissed.

I was completely taken aback. I would never not honor him. I would never not respect him. Of all the humans I knew, I probably respected him the most.

"How arrogant and self-centered," she added as I sat there with tears rolling down my cheeks. She had indeed hit a nerve. She was a good friend.

I realized that I had arrogantly focused on the honor and felt inadequate when my real focus should have been the responsibility and the possibility to be of service.

I had been arrogant and disrespectful for believing I was inadequate. Not only had I insulted Fools Crow, I had insulted the Creator who created me. My fears and self-centeredness were keeping me from fulfilling my responsibilities to Fools Crow, the Creator, and all my relations.

We must remember that all relationships are sacred.

Participating in the Process of Relationships

It is clear that we cannot have a good relationships unless we are relating to our spirituality in a good way.

Relationships require that we have two active infinity processes that we can conceptualize as infinity signs pulsing within us at all times. The first infinity process and one that is necessary for us to have any other type of relationship is an infinity pulsing process between us and our Great Spirit. For my own Western-trained mind, I see it as a vertical infinity sign that starts at our feet, crosses in our solar plexus, and connects to the Infinite through our heads. The other pulsing infinity process is one that goes out of our heart chakra to another person's, many people's, a group's, or all our relations' solar plexuses and it moves up the body to the heart chakra and is then sent out to the other's solar plexus where it moves up the heart chakra and so the process goes on infinitely. When the energy enters our solar plexus, we take out some of the love we receive. As it moves up to our heart we add more love to it, so when we send it back there is even more love. As it enters the other's solar plexus, they take out some love, add more as it moves up their body, and send back more. Meanwhile, the Creator keeps adding an infinite supply. There is plenty of love for everybody.

This infinity sign is very fragile between people. We can be resentful and not send it to the other. We can be angry and not let it in. We can be greedy and try to take all the love and not add to it. We can be out of balance with the Creator and not have a good supply. We can be guarded and full of pain and not let it in. This infinity process, this pulsing through all our relations, is powerful and fragile at the same time.

We, as a species, have a great responsibility to keep these energy flows clean and functioning. From my experience, our ancestors were much better at this than we have become and I trust that with their help we can return to a more balanced universe.

It is clear that we need to be honest in our relationships. We live in a culture where honesty, when it occurs, is often experienced as shocking. We are so accustomed to "spin," control, manipulation, out-and-out lies, and being managed, that many of us have forgotten how to be honest in a good way.

In my experience, dishonesty is always destructive. Honesty may hurt, it may be painful, and we may not like it, and, if we are honest about ourselves, it is never destructive.

Jesus said, "You shall know the truth and the truth shall set you free." That has been my experience.

Our ancestors were so unaccustomed to any sort of dishonesty that we Native people still have an inherent disbelief in dishonesty in people we like and want to trust. Luckily, we still believe that honesty is possible and preferable. And, we would rather say nothing than be dishonest. For those seeking to return to our roots, relearning to be honest and developing a dishonesty detection gene can help. When we know we are being lied to we find it much easier than letting ourselves be duped. Sometimes, I *know* in my gut what it was like for my ancestors when they first encountered dishonesty—not pleasant!

"Managing" others has become quite an admired skill in today's culture. Managing is just another word for manipulation. In the dominant culture when the behavior connected to one word becomes too obviously obnoxious and destructive, we find a new word.

My experience is that people don't like to be managed or manipulated, and they don't trust or like the people who do it regardless of how skilled they are.

In order to make a paradigm shift and return to the teachings of our ancestors, we need to be more conscious of what we are doing for, with, and in our relationships.

Relationships are energy. We cannot do them in our heads with our thinking, and the way we do them is key to our ability to *be* Native.

Relationships are key processes that can help us return to our being.

Never, never should we be abusive or accept abuse in our relationships—no matter what!

No discussion about relationships is complete without mentioning making love. For the Cherokee, making love, which includes sexual love, would never be used for selfishness, exploitation, power, or control. It is just too sacred. Our ancestors made love all the time in many ways.

Making love, like all that has been given us, is a gift of the Creator and is sacred. Whenever we defile the sacred, we are spitting in the face of the Creator.

Making love is an opportunity that we have been given to experience loving at a very deep level. Making love is a form of intimacy that most closely gives us the experience and a vague approximation of the intensity of the love that exists between ourselves and the Creator.

There are many forms of making love. Doing dishes together can be making love. We can make love as an everyday thing. Sexual love is only a deeper level of an ongoing loving relationship.

During sex, we have the opportunity to lose the focus on self and focus on loving and giving pleasure to another person on the deepest level. Sex offers us one of the greatest opportunities we have as humans to go beyond self and connect on the deepest levels beyond ourselves. The moment of a full and complete orgasm is a loss of self that can be the most intense level of loss of self that humans experience. For a Cherokee, to profane this process suggests such a loss of connection with the sacred that it is devastating to us.

Even using sex to "make a child" is a misuse of sex. There is no way we can experience the abandon of self that is needed to connect with the Creator when we have an agenda for our lovemaking.

The Creator may give us the gift of a child, and that child can best be nurtured when it comes out of committed, selfless loving.

I had a dream once where I *knew* this kind of loving on a very intense level. I was visiting a Maori Kuia friend in New Zealand. I dreamed that I was in a kind of community of mixed people. We were expecting visitors and the others and I were busy preparing for their arrival.

When they arrived, I felt the sacredness of their leader on a very profound level. He was so beautiful that I just wanted to stare at him. He reminded me of my concept of Jesus, yet he was not like the usual pictures. His beauty was holy and it radiated everywhere. I continued to serve him and others until it was time for bed. He kept moving among us and talking to everyone. We had no direct verbal communication and yet, I felt he *knew* me.

As the evening wore on, people began to lay down their pallets to sleep Marae style (everyone sleeping in one big room together). I lost track of him and, being tired, rolled out my bed roll, turned on my left side (I always sleep on my side), and immediately started to fall asleep. Suddenly, I felt myself spooned by another person. I knew it was he. It was not sexual as in our limited way of defining sexual. I then felt the most intense loving I have felt in my life. I not only experienced this intensity in my body, it completely filled my mind and spirit too. The intensity of the loving was so profound and potent that I could feel every cell of my physical and spiritual body reverberating with it. (I have known approximations of this experience when making love and it was nothing like the intensity of this experience.)

The intensity was so great that I woke myself up. I simply could not stand it. I sat with my feelings for a while in the middle of the night and knew that I had just had one of the most profound experiences of my life and had been given a great learning. One aspect of that learning was that we, as humans, probably do not have the physical capability to experience the completeness of the love of the Creator. We have accepted many limitations being on this physical plane and this is one of them. Sex is, or can and should be, the best approximation we have. And when we exploit our sexual lovemaking in any way, we lose this opportunity. I had always known this from my teachings and this dream helped me know and feel this reality at a different level.

In the morning, I told my Kuia host about my dream. She listened intently and then said, "Oh yes, that was Tane [the Maori word for the male aspect of God]. He often visits people who are guests here."

I knew she was right.

In the Bible, there are three words for love. *Eros, philos,* and *agape.* Eros is likened to physical love, philos is likened to brotherly love, and agape is likened to the love of God.

Often in the Bible when they talk about sexual *loving* it is not just eros. In some of the older translations sexual love was described in the terms "he *knew* her." To "know" someone is to experience them on a physical, emotional, and spiritual level. Making love as our elders taught us is physical, emotional, and connects us with our experience of "knowing" the Creator. "Techniques" will never cut it. When we are ready and have grown in ourselves and our relationship, we can possibly be ready to make love.

Making love is a matter of the highest integrity and ultimate relationship and can be present in every form of relating.

Aunty Margaret, the great Kahuna of Lomi Lomi, has said: "You should make love with a righteous man every day,"—"righteous" being the key word here. Making love is good for us when it comes out of our spiritual being.

Our being in relationship with everything is key to returning to the call of our ancestral blood.

The Fifth Process

Honor and Respect

WHEN I WAS A CHILD, for the first three years of my life, my great-grandmother, Mary Elizabeth, was my primary parent and the adult who spent the most time with me. She taught me honor and respect by example.

My earliest memory is her bathing me in a big tub in the living room where it was warm. She would never use a washcloth because she said that they were "too rough." She used a piece of an old well-worn sheet, which was so soft it caressed my skin. Her washing of me was so gentle, so loving, and so respectful that, to this day, I can still feel the gentleness of that cloth on my skin. Her drying of me was never rough or rushed as she wrapped me in a big soft towel and then gently pulled my warmed flannel nightie over my head. I then quickly padded to the bedroom where a big fluffed-up featherbed that had been warmed by a hot brick awaited me. I loved jumping into that bed, but not before I sat on the chair beside the bed and held my feet out so she could gently wipe them off with a warm, soft cloth.

"We do not want to carry any dust of the day into our bed, do we?" she would say as she wiped my feet.

We then said our prayers and I was tucked in. Tucking in was always a ritual in our family. The whole ritual was full of honor and respect.

She was completely respectful of me as she prepared me for bed. There was no haste or pressure. The process of the preparation was respected over the completion of the task. It took as long as it took and every gesture, movement, and word was full of love and respect.

Our prayers honored everyone in our lives, the many gifts we had received that day and all creation. She treated me with respect, and I reciprocated in kind. The whole process ended the day with honor, respect, and balance.

The water was honored and respected. The process of bathing was honored and respected. My body was honored and respected. The bed was honored and respected. My sleep was honored and respected. Without any words, she taught me that all these rituals and all the process of all life were to be honored and respected.

I could see and feel that same honor and respect in the way she folded the clothes after they were lovingly washed. I could see that same honor and respect in the way she approached and prepared the food.

We lived in a state of gratitude because it was crystal clear to my great-grandmother that everything we had—everything!—including life itself—was a gift from the Creator.

We had not earned all these gifts. We were not *entitled* to all these gifts. They were gifts. We could show our gratitude by honoring and respecting all creation.

As a child, I knew that I was honored and respected. I was in a constant state of learning. My great-grandmother, my grandparents, my parents, my uncles, and all the people of our little town in Oklahoma took it upon themselves to honor and respect me by being my constant teachers and sharing their particular knowledge. I was the only grandchild for many years so I had a very rich and busy "classroom" in which I learned by example, watching, and participating. I learned that one folds clean clothes with loving care and gratitude. I learned to wash dishes with presence, loving care, and gratitude.

I loved to watch my great-grandmother comb her long silvery-golden tinted hair. It was so long that it exceeded the length of her arm. She would comb it to arm's length and then gently pull it through the comb.

As she grew older I rejoiced in combing her hair with the same honor and respect she had shown in combing mine when I was a child.

When we walked to the country store, we always cleaned up before we went—respecting ourselves and others—and I was always impressed with the gentleness with which she approached people and the honor and respect they showed her as a medicine person and one who cared for their pain and illnesses.

She would take me with her when she gathered medicines in the meadows and woods, and she gathered and dug with the same gentleness that she had shown in wiping the dust off my feet after my bath.

She rarely uttered the words *honor* and *respect*. She didn't have to. She lived them.

I have often heard people from the dominant society in a derogatory way say that Native people were sun worshippers, or worshipped nature, or worshipped the earth. That is just not my experience.

In fact, I have come to believe that "worshipping" is peculiarly non-Native and connected with the revealed religions and a belief in hierarchy.

I did not see my elders "worshipping" except in Christian churches (even then in a different way than the "white" way). Worship seems to be based and centered on a hierarchical worldview, which I have not experienced in Native peoples the world over.

I remember one of my elders and teachers, Lee Piper, saying to me, "We Tsa La Gi don't bow our head when we pray. That is not respectful. The Creator wants us to look him straight in the eye for we are one with the Creator."

I have found not bowing my head when praying very difficult after all my training in Christianity.

As I grew in wisdom, I could see that we Native people did not *worship* the earth, the sun, or nature. We were rightfully grateful for all the gifts that each constantly gave us and we honored and respected them for that. At some point as an adult, it just was so logical and made so much sense to me that all that we have comes from the earth, the sky, the water, and the sun. It is, indeed, logical to show our gratitude by honoring and respecting all of them.

When I sit with the old ones, I can see that they have much pain because they have the wisdom about how all that we have comes from the earth, the water, and the sun, and we have not been able to protect them as we should have.

They say to me that we need to awaken the blood and wisdom of our ancestors to bring forth the honor and respect of the planet and nature. It is time that we again learn to live out of honor and respect in all that we do.

It has become clear to me that, as we return to honoring and respecting our elders and participate in that process on a daily, moment-to-moment basis, our brains become less foggy, our eyes get less hazy, and that process of honoring and respecting The All returns us to balance.

We cannot honor and respect in hierarchy. It is only out of seeing our oneness and our interconnectedness that we return to honor and respect.

My mother was a great teacher in seeing and honoring and respecting all people. She did not have a prejudiced bone in her body at a time in the South when racial prejudice was the cultural norm. She was so deeply steeped in the Cherokee knowledge of the oneness that she completely lived out of that awareness. Living out of this awareness is what I mean about *being* Native.

When I was little, we lived in Fayetteville, Arkansas. "Home" was still Oklahoma where my uncles, grandparents, and great-grandmother were, and we had moved to Fayetteville because my father had found work there.

We lived a few blocks from the town square and every day Mother and I would walk to the square and around it. Although we had little spare money (it was in the 1930s, coming out of the Great Depression), Mother had befriended a disabled boy who sold pencils on the street corner. Mother always said that, as a part of the whole, it is our responsibility to care for those less fortunate than ourselves. We would chat with this young man, and Mother would buy a pencil or give him a nickel, which was a lot in those days, and certainly a lot for us!

One day as we approached his corner we could see a gang of teenagers (four or five as I remember) teasing him, picking on him, scattering his pencils, and generally harassing him.

Now, it is important to remember that my mother was a short woman—about five feet four inches. I saw her rise up to eight feet tall and take on the whole bunch. She grabbed a couple of those teenagers by the nape of the neck and literally lifted them off the ground. She spoke to them all in a voice of authority I had never heard before and said, "Shame on you and shame on your parents. Have they not taught you how to behave? How could you treat this wonderful young man this way? Are you not grateful for the gifts you have?"

She looked at and through them at the same time. I had never seen her so powerful. Then, she set the two of them down and said, "Now apologize, pick up all the pencils you have scattered, and pay him for any you have damaged." She crossed her arms and stood there with that "gaze."

I was in awe of her and so deeply proud of her at that moment. It reminded me of the story of Jesus and the money changers in the temple. (We Cherokee were good Christians too. We honored all paths to the Creator equally.)

The boys apologized, cleaned up the mess, paid for damaged pencils, and left with my mother's words—"There, now don't you feel better about yourself?"—ringing in their ears.

Then, Mother shrank back to her normal self and chatted with the young man who sold the pencils.

"Thank you, ma'am," he said.

"Oh, it was nothing," said Mother. "Any decent person would have done the same thing."

She bought her usual pencil and we continued our walk. And she murmured to me, "Poor kids, their parents have not taught them what's important. We will pray for them."

I learned a great deal about honor and respect that day. I also learned that when we are doing the work of the Creator and following the teachings of our ancestors, we will have the strength to do what is right.

Participating in the Process of Honor and Respect

The basic concepts and concomitant processes of honor and respect are almost absent in current culture. Even people who should know better don't seem to act in a way that would indicate that they remember.

We see celebrity worship, Jesus worship, Allah worship, all often devoid of honor and respect. We see nature being crushed under our materialism and greed, and we long for some honor and respect out there. I was taught that everything in creation is equally important in the eyes of God and should be treated as such. There are those who know more than I do about almost everything and those who know less. That is as it should be. Yet, on a higher level, we are all equally part of the same creation. There are those who have more money, power, and prestige. And, those who have less. That is also as it should be. Yet, as part of the whole, we are all equal. When we honor and respect others for who and what they are and know we are equal in the eyes of God, we are *being* Native. When we go one up or one down with anyone, we are breaking our covenant with the Creator.

Fortunately, we can only change ourselves; we need to return to the teachings of our ancestors and start practicing honor and respect "in here"—in our own hearts.

How might your life change if you started to:
1) Treat all elders with honor and respect?
2) Fold your laundry with honor and respect?
3) Treat your pots and pans with honor and respect?
4) Honor each piece of food with gratitude, honor, and respect?
5) Treat all your relationships with honor and respect?
6) Respect the time and the place—wherever you find yourself.
7) Give thanks for all you have to enjoy around you.

Just try it.

You'll feel better about yourself. And, your ancestors will be smiling.

Remember, being Native comes from the inside out. Yet, the outside behavior can help mold our insides. It's all a process and a whole.

Honor and respect are key to all relationships.

The Sixth Process

Nature

WE ARE NOT ABOVE OR DETACHED FROM NATURE. We are a part of nature. When we convince ourselves that we are different from, or not a part of, something—anything, anyone—we feel we have license to manipulate, exploit, desecrate, abuse, devour, and destroy it. We have developed deceiving ourselves into a national art and pastime. We have done this to a point where we have convinced ourselves that we are above nature, more important than nature, and it is all right for us to exploit, use, and devour all creation. We have been taught that the human and the human mind are the highest forms of intelligence and consciousness. Whether we are talking about relationships, products, or nature, the process is the same.

Our ancestors and our elders weep that, as we move away from honor and respect, we embrace abuse and exploitation. What we have become easy or at least complacent with in ourselves and our relationships we have become even more comfortable with in doing to nature.

When I convince myself that I am not nature, I can exploit it. When I can convince myself that the Arab or Muslim is not my family, I can murder him or her with impunity.

When I let myself realize that I am both part of nature and inextricably one in all of creation, I have to deal with myself and the other with more of myself.

We are not above nature; we cannot detach from Nature. We are one with nature and a participating part of nature. We need nature and nature needs us.

As Witi Ihimaera wrote in his book *Tangi*, "The rhythm of the land and the rhythm of his blood had been one and the same. And he had begun the planting and both blood and land had gradually become calm."

Whether we like it or not, we are in a relationship with nature, and it behooves us not to be abusers and exploiters.

Phil Lane Sr., a Yankton Sioux elder and spiritual leader, once said to me, "Whenever you lose your way, when you feel lost, and have lost your connection with the Creator, go into Nature. Put your face and mouth against your Mother, the Earth's, breast. She will nurture you, she will heal you. She is there waiting for you. You need only to go to her."

Rolling Thunder, a Cherokee medicine man, once said to me, "When you are ready, come to me, I will take you into nature. You can learn everything you need to learn in nature."

Nature is one of our best teachers and can heal us when nothing else works.

One of the saddest experiences I have ever had is when a group of city American Indian kids came to one of my workshops in Big Sky, Montana. One of their adult leaders thought it would be good for them to get out in nature.

They were absolutely terrified. When we talked, they said that they were comfortable in the city and knew how to survive in the city. They did not know how to make it in nature. I was shocked beyond belief. I had never put the words *American Indian* and *fear of nature* in the same sentence. So effective was the American Indian *relocation* process that we have much to do to help our children and grandchildren return to their knowings.

Everything that we have comes from nature. Our houses, our cars, our clothes, our furniture. The more "refined" a thing is, the more the power of its "nature" is difficult to experience.

I had a friend once who was a Mohican. His work called him to live and work in New York City. We kept contact during his tenure in the city and talked often. Each time we talked, I could see that he was doing a good job and yet, inside, he was dying. I wrote a poem about his Indian soul withering as he was encased in concrete, steel, and asphalt. He began to develop physical and emotional problems. I kept telling him that he needed to get out in nature. Finally, he was transferred to Hawaii, in my experience, a place where Nature demands that you live *with* and *in* her. Slowly, over the years, I could see that the pieces of his soul were coming back together again.

Hawaii is a place where many American Indians come to pull in the shards and fragments of their souls that have been far-flung out into the universe, waiting until they can return to their rightful place.

In Hawaii, it is impossible to ignore nature and even more impossible not to live with nature. As hard as Western culture has tried to impose its detachment from nature by building tall buildings with windows that do not open and wasting resources on heating and air conditioning, nature eventually wins out in Hawaii.

You can plan to go to the beach on Saturday, but it is pouring rain with gale-force winds. Monday, on the other hand, is a perfect beach day.

Your office can allot two hours off for the funeral of a family member, but the funeral lasts for four days.

You can crave peaches from the mainland, but the lychee tree right outside your door is loaded with the biggest, sweetest, most tantalizing lychees that are beyond delicious. When they are chilled, that one bite into their sweet fruit makes the image of peaches completely disappear. Nature is everywhere and quite active.

You can hate the way the wild pigs dig up your yard and the carefully planned garden. Yet, when the old sow and nine little piglets appear the next day, you immediately think: "Aren't they cute? The yard and the garden will grow back. We need our wild pigs."

I am so grateful that Hawaii has not moved as far from nature as the mainland has, and it welcomed me when I needed to heal and return to my Native roots.

No matter where we are, nature is there and welcomes us back to participate in her wholeness.

My son lived in Los Angeles, a difficult place to live at best. He had chosen a tree-lined community street not too far from the beach and, still, he needs to escape to the rawness of nature to recollect his Native soul.

He recently described to me how he felt riding his motorcycle up an old logging trail into the mountains, lying down on a picnic table in an abandoned campground on the top of the mountain, looking up through the trees, and watching the clouds. He came back a different person.

In my early years, growing up in rural Arkansas and Oklahoma, nature was simply, unquestionably part of my daily existence. My great-grandmother taught me to respect how nature provided for our needs. She taught me what plants to use for teas, poultices, chewing, holding in the mouth, or grinding into a powder to put on our food. She taught me to look at each plant, leaf, root, and stem with honor and respect. She taught me the interrelatedness of the plants and the animals, and how much humans were less clear about ourselves and needed our plant and animal relations.

She taught me that often sitting with my back against a tree and quietly "waiting with" what the tree could tell me was the right medicine at times.

I saw her gather and dig her medicines with such honor and respect that it brings tears to my eyes to remember that frail body stooping over or sitting on the ground to receive what nature had to give to us when we needed it.

I grew up knowing that nature had and would provide all I needed. What a comfort that has always been to me. That certain knowing is like a security blanket that always wraps me. I know that if all else fails, I can live with and off the land.

I hunted and fished with my father, gathered medicines with my great-grandmother, and gathered food with my mother. Nature and my constant enduring relationship with the Great Spirit have given me the serenity I need to deal with life. Whenever I temporarily forget who I am and where I belong, I return to nature and come back in balance with myself, my Creator, and the universe.

There is an old Zen saying that rocks are just people who sat Zen for a very long time. My elders always told me to "listen to the rocks." They said that the rocks had been here longer than any of us and had gathered great knowledge. Listening to a rock doesn't make much sense to a Western mind. It makes infinite sense to a Native mind.

Participating in the Process of Nature

It is impossible to participate in the process of anything if we are detached from it and/or feel superior to it. Seeing and knowing our complete dependence upon nature helps us move from superiority and detachment to honor and respect. Participation comes later. When we begin to see the brilliance of a tree or of a rock, this helps us to begin to develop some humility.

I will never forget the first time I saw a redwood tree. I was five years old. I had never seen anything as majestic and awe inspiring. No cathedral or monument can hold a candle to a redwood. I return to the redwoods again and again. I need to. They put me in my place. I have tree friends all over the world. I remember seeing a redwood that had been cut out at the bottom (that gave me pain) so a car could drive through it, and it was still living!

I remember seeing a crosscut of a huge Redwood and in its rings were marked significant events in many hundreds of years of human history. Whew! Who do we think we are?

Walking on the earth in moccasins is a very different experience than walking on the earth with shoes.

To participate in the process of nature, we have to approach her with great humility.

I have found it good to live in nature, and I am grateful that I have that opportunity.

Don't just walk through nature. I know several people who obsessively take long brisk walks, and the walks seem to be all about *them*, with no possibility to be in and affected by nature.

Bring nature to you if you aren't in nature as much as you need to be.

Surround yourself with rocks. Touch and feel them. Get to know them. Take time with them. Learn to listen to them. Beware of interpreting them.

Ground yourself with flowers and plants. Let them do their magic on you. Express your gratitude daily for all that nature gives you.

Be aware that your food is nature and is providing for all your physical needs and accept that you need the trees much more than they need you.

Sit and watch a thunderstorm move across the horizon. Participating in the process of Nature will take time—time away from the "important" things you have been doing.

Let nature feed your soul. Rarely, if ever, do the tasks we are so busy completing nourish our souls like nature does.

Are you afraid of nature? Accept those fears and talk to her about them.

I find it so important to have tree friends. Sitting with my back against a tree and listening is an experience like no other.

I used to own a piece of land on Orcas in the San Juan Islands in Puget Sound. There was one big cedar on that property that I just *loved*. It was so sturdy, so powerful, so beautiful that I returned to that tree again and again.

I was describing it to a friend of mine and she immediately said, "Oh, that must be the tree where the queen of the fairies lives!"

I was so excited! My mother had a great relationship with the little people, put out food for them, and willingly accepted their help in all sorts of situations. Her Irish part honored the fairies and the leprechauns. Her Cherokee blood always spoke of the little people. I was thrilled with the possibility.

I sat with my back against that big old cedar and implored the queen of the fairies to let me see her. I had envisioned that she would be in a long, blue, sparkling dress with long hair.

After a long time of prayer, imploring, and silence, I opened my eyes and—THERE SHE WAS—in a long *green* dress, with a broad smile on her face and her eyes lovingly looking at me.

"Yes, I live here," she said. "I'm so glad you love this tree. We protect you always. As for the green dress, if I had had a blue dress, you would not have believed in me. Your scientific mind would have deducted that I was a figment of your imagination."

Her humor reminded me of my Cherokee family's.

Nature can hold many exciting surprises for us if we but let her in.

The Seventh Process

Process and Participation

WE DO NOT LIVE IN A STATIC WORLD. We are a process. We are not an entity. We are a process. Everything around us screams of process. The trees are a process. Our gardens are a process. Our children are each a process—a unique process—like the snowflakes. Our societies are a process. Nature is a process. Some of our greatest frustrations and pain arise when we try to make ourselves, our relationships, and our world static. Much of the focus on "fixing" comes out of our Western scientific paradigm which focuses on measurement > prediction > control.

At one point, when I was writing about living in process, my editor told me that I needed to define process. I was shocked. How does one define a universal truth? One does not define a universal truth. It is known.

Defining process is like defining "spiritual" when everything is spirit. We would like God-The-Creator to be static so we would feel secure, and everything in creation tells us that God-The-Creator is a process like all creation shows us.

"Everyone knows what process is," I replied from my Native being.

"No they don't," she replied. "You need to define it."

I hate definitions. They are so static!

So, I went home and asked members of my family and people who had studied with me if they knew what process was.

To a person, they answered—"I'm not really sure . . . ?"

Luckily, I was off to Hawaii, so I shared this experience with some of my Hawaiian family. They were as shocked as I was. "Do you know what process is?" I asked a bit timidly. They looked shocked again. "Of course we do!" they shot back.

"Everything is process. Process is everything. All life is process."

We shook our heads slowly.

"How sad," my Hawaiian friends said. "How very sad. We must pray for them."

Again, I felt more connectedness with my Hawaiian family and their worldview than I did with my white brothers and sisters. With my white family, we were looking at the same world and our eyes saw something completely different.

I never have come up with a definition, yet I know and experience the fullness of ever-present process.

Barry Stevens, an elder who helped develop gestalt therapy, was a friend of mine. She wrote a book called *Don't Push the River* with a subtitle of *It Flows by Itself*. She would talk about our entering the river and floating along with the process of the river. If we fight the river, we have more difficulty. If we float with it, life carries us. I knew she was on to something and I sensed there was more.

Life gets better when we know we *are* the river. We aren't passengers on the river. We *are* the river. It is when we know that our place on this planet is not to control our lives and the lives of those around us, but to participate where we are with who we are that our lives begin to evolve and change.

We cannot control our lives, people, places or things, our children, our spouses, our jobs, the economy, or much of anything. Much illness and grief ensue when we try. We can participate as fully as we can in the processes the Creator presents to us, and in so doing our lives unfold. Some call it living life on life's terms.

My great-grandmother was very good at helping me learn this truth about the ever-presence of process and participating with it.

We would go into the garden together to let it tell us what we would have for dinner. I loved these forays into our garden.

"Oh, Grandma," I would say. "Can we have some corn for dinner?"

"Perhaps," she would say. "Let's see what the corn has to say about that. Selu has much to say about many things."

We would walk in the garden and feel the ears.

"What do you feel, Elizabeth Anne?" she would ask. I focused on feeling what I felt as I checked out the ear of corn.

"It feels small, Grandma. I don't feel the kernels."

"Do you think it is ready for us to eat it?" she would ask.

"No, Grandma, it is not ready," I replied.

"Let's try another," she would say.

At the end of our journey through the cornfield, we would know if the corn was ready to feed us that evening.

If it weren't, in the process of checking the corn we might also have checked the green beans and they seemed quite happy to feed us that evening.

She, in every day, in every way, was teaching me about process. She was teaching me to be respectful of everyone's and everything's process, and she was teaching me to honor all process. We would have a lovely supper with ham and green beans from the garden, looking forward to eating corn when it had completed its ripening process.

She never mentioned the word *process,* she lived it.

At night, I was often of the opinion that it was not time for me to go to bed. I can't ever remember her saying, "It is time, you have to go to bed now." She respected my process.

She always said something like, "I tell you what, let's get your bath and get ready for bed. Then, we'll crawl in bed and I will read to you a bit, and we'll see if you need to stay awake for awhile."

I never lasted more than a couple paragraphs. She taught me to respect my sleep process. To this day, I let the process of my body tell me when I am tired and need sleep. There are times I need to tell my body that it needs to keep going for a while, and I always let my body know I have heard it and will rest as soon as possible. Often, fifteen minutes is enough.

My great-grandmother was a process coach.

As I look back over my life, I can see that it functioned best when I participated in the process of my life and did not try to make it look and feel like I thought it should.

All too often, external circumstances and other people's agendas try to force me out of being the river of my life. Whenever I let that happen, I suffer and so do others.

Living my process is never self-centered or harmful to others. Trying to impose my agendas upon myself or others always is.

Let's face it, there are just times when we simply don't have all the information. When we trust the process, we will know when to act, and often it is not in a direction we thought it would be.

Sigh! We just can't know everything.

We can participate to the best of our ability.

Participating in the Process of Process and Participation

Remember I told you that in learning to *be* Native there would often be a sensation of moving in circles?

Living in process and participation in our living process may be one of the most difficult aspects of becoming Native.

The illusion of control permeates the belief system of Western culture. Almost everything is about control. No wonder we see such confusion, low self-esteem, and anger. How frustrating it is to fail at trying to control things we can't control and then to be held responsible (at least by ourselves!) for our not being able to control them!

How senseless.

The illusion of control has no place in returning to the wisdom of our ancestors. Like the story of our elders hiding the wisdom inside of us, we can plant seeds and we have to trust that they have their own process, guided by a wisdom greater than ours.

That's just the way it is.

The Eighth Process

Honesty

Our old people were often described by the white people as inscrutable. I know they were often silent around people of the dominant culture.

In my experience there were other very strong factors operating: 1) They were often shocked beyond belief with the behavior, thinking, assumptions, and worldview of those people unlike themselves. 2) They were an amazingly honest people. 3) They functioned out of a level of respect and politeness that is not even imaginable in today's culture.

Unfortunately, some of their descendants are not quite so polite.

I include myself in this latter group, although as I mature, I'm getting better.

I have never been with an elder who didn't impress me with her or his honest relationship with the Great Spirit. Of course we cannot fool the Great Spirit. What a silly thought!

Yet I see many people try.

What I love about being with elders is the respectful, easy, honest, and accepting way they have of relating to their Creator. This relationship is an honest relationship. They are not arguing with, trying to manipulate and control, or wrestling with their Higher Power. They are just honest and accepting.

I love the way elders say, "Well, I don't know much about that" or "I have some knowledge about that" or "I actually was taught something about it by a very wise person."

It's not here or there. It's just the truth.

When I was growing up, and to this day, I have been accused of lacking humility, bragging, or being arrogant when I say I am good at something. I have developed the response, "I'm not bragging. I'm just telling the truth. I am just as likely to say, 'I know nothing about that' when I don't, or, 'I know a little bit, and I wouldn't trust me on that if I were you.'"

I have found that in this society, there is some valor assigned to saying you are not good at something when you and others know you are. I would much rather err in the direction of honesty than false humility when given the choice.

My experience with Native elders is that they do not miss much (very little, in fact) and they are astute judges as to how and when to say something. They do not open their mouths if they do not experience open ears to receive their teachings and message.

Their honesty is conservative and considerate. Why waste time when someone is not ready to hear?

I always experience elders being honest about themselves. Deception is never worth it.

I don't know whether my great-grandmother said this explicitly, and what I heard from all my family was that to be dishonest was to run the risk of rupturing my relationship with the Creator. What could ever be worth taking that risk?

I remember hearing, "If you can't say something nice, don't say anything at all."

Hence, the inscrutability. My experience is that the old ones were respect-ful beyond belief and with whites often found it very difficult to say something "nice." So they said nothing.

What do you say to a people who smoke the sacred pipe with you, make agreements, swear sacred oaths, in good faith and by smoking the pipe together affirm our oneness, our familiness, and then keep not one of those sacred oaths? For an honest people, the only answer is shocked silence.

Our silence has held for hundreds of years. Yet we have been watching and waiting and planting our seeds. We knew that a time would come when the Creator would require our people, our seventh generation, to speak out with the wisdom of the ancients and the experience of cross-racial people. Our elders knew that there would come a time when our people needed to come forth with the honesty of our tribal wisdom and the skill to speak with those who need to know in a way all could understand. That time is now.

In order for our people to speak out in a way to be heard, we need to show the respect, the ability to demonstrate our living out of the whole-ness and the wisdom of our ancients. This must be balanced with the honesty about the seriousness and importance of this ancient wisdom. Its coming forth is vital to our survival. We have to be living out of these twenty-one processes. We need to then describe and articulate them with honesty, compassion, power—and clarity. What we say when we speak needs to come out of the soul of our being.

We cannot do what is needed unless we are honest with ourselves. That kind of honesty takes courage and clarity—and time.

An Irish elder once said to me, "God made time—and He made plenty of it."

We have all the time we need to learn what we need to learn to speak from our *being* Native. All we need is to be on the path.

Participating in the Process of Honesty

Learning honesty in a society that supports and even demands dishonesty is, of course, not easy.

We have to learn when, where, and how to be honest. With ourselves, we need always to be honest. We need support groups of people with whom we can be honest. And, we need to practice honesty in all our affairs.

Sometimes, our most honest position is to say nothing as our ancestors have done. And, there are times when we have to speak out as individuals and in groups.

The Creator will lead us. All we need to do is have the skills when the time is right.

The Ninth Process

The Process of Co-Creating

WHEN WE SEE AND UNDERSTAND that we are part of nature and all creation, we begin to understand at a deep spiritual level that we are responsible. We are responsible for much more than ourselves, our immediate families, and our own personal lives. In fact, we begin to let go of the illusion of a personal life. We begin to experience that we not only are responsible for the co-destruction of our universe, we are responsible for co-creating our universe.

Our old ones taught us that when we walk softly on the land we help co-create a beautiful world for all of us. We can co-create a beautiful world that is healthy for all our relations—human, plant, animal, earth—and we can co-destroy. It is up to all of us, and we have a responsibility to make informed decisions at every step along the way. When we treat our material possessions with care and understanding, they reward us by lasting and serving us longer. Hence, we do not have to use up the resources of the planet so fast. Planned obsolescence is not a part of the consciousness of our elders. Planned care and conservation are part of the consciousness we have sleeping in our genes.

I remember my great-grandmother saying to me, "Elizabeth Anne, take care of your toys and then you will have them forever."

"Why would I want them forever, Grandma?" I would ask.

"So you can have the pleasure of seeing your great-grandchildren playing with them as I am now," she would respond with love and tears glistening in her eyes.

81

"Ah," I said. And I can still feel the love I felt for her and the toys at that moment. It was a kind of reverence for those toys that I imagined had been so special to her as a child years and years before I was born. I was so grateful that she had taken care of them. I still have two of her china-headed dolls that were special to my children too. They will be passed on.

As I was having fun with these toys, they were teaching me reverence. These are the things we have the opportunity to pass on to our children—not just the toys, but also the feeling that goes with the toys.

We can make a beautiful world and protect and assist nature, we can ignore our world, or we can actively destroy our world around us. It is up to us. It is our choice. Are we protecting the species of animals we have around us? Are we creating a world where new species can evolve and thrive?

Greed is one of the most powerful forces that interferes with our co-creating. When we want more and more materially, we are willing to destroy our planet to get it.

Mining is a good example of our co-destruction. When we overmine, we take out of the earth elements that are necessary for its balance. Not only are we taking out and not replenishing, we open up a possibility for toxic elements that have been protected by the earth's crust to spew out into our groundwater and soil.

I saw a TV program once on the effects of one hundred years of mining in Colorado. It was about the Superfund program that is making an effort to clean up after extensive mining in various parts of the country.

"Are you making progress?" the reporter asked the scientist.

"Yes," she answered. "But there is always more."

"How long will it take?" asked the reporter.

The scientist paused. "As long as there is human life on this planet," was her response.

I felt sick as I heard this.

What has our greed done to the generations that come after us? Did we consider that when we opened up huge gaping holes in the earth to take out what we wanted? Did we consider the aftermath when we allowed offshore oil drilling?

What are we co-creating in every moment of our lives?

When we see ourselves as co-creators of the world around us, or co-creators of the people our children become, or as we are working with the trees and animals in our lives, we approach our responsibility in a different way.

Now let me be clear about this process of co-creating. No traditional Native person would ever see herself or himself as being God in any way. This difference between ourselves and God is completely clear to a Native person. There is no belief that we can or should be able to control anything. Controlling is just, quite simply, not our job, and we do not need to concern ourselves with such a foolish notion. We only have to participate and trust the outcome. Trying to control other people, places, or things is a confusing idea to a Native mind—confusing and foolish.

Participating in the Process of Co-creating

As you evolve into someone in the process of being responsive to the call of your Native blood, are you becoming aware of your own comfort with whatever usury and greed has developed in your life over the years?

In responding to the call of our Native blood we may see that there may be some aspects of the way we have been living that have been co-destructive of ourselves and the world around us, that we might come to want to move away from. Our old ones never ask us to let go of anything that is spiritually good for us.

How might we move from usury to participating and co-creating?

We might start by asking ourselves, "Is this good for the next seven generations and beyond?" If not, it shouldn't be done.

The Tenth Process

Valuing Differences

"But Grandmother," questioned the young Ojibway woman about the coming of the white people, "there were more of you, you could have killed them or driven them back. Why did you let them stay?"

The old woman was silent for what seemed to be an eternity to the young woman. Then, she looked up with a sadness that was ancient.

"Because they needed us," came the soft reply.

Our old ones had such a broader perspective than we often do from our snail's eye view.

Our people have always respected the eagle who flies higher than any other bird and therefore has a perspective that is vaster and wider than any creature that is earth-bound can possibly have. There are always some among us who fly with and listen to the perspective of the eagle. Eagles see any situation a notch or two or three or a hundred up from those who focus on themselves and their world.

The old grandmother who said, "Because they needed us," was one of the eagle people.

Those who live out of a snail's eye view are fearful of differences. Differences are perceived as a threat and are to be annihilated at all costs. Any worldview that is based upon manipulation and control is fearful of differences.

It is easy to see how a people who saw all creation as a whole would value and even seek out differences. They saw all people as family and believed, in great humility, that none of us has the whole picture of reality and that we needed one another to put the puzzle together better to understand the whole. With open minds and hearts, our old ones welcomed the newcomers assuming that the newcomers, like they, would eagerly respect and embrace them, because both groups had something to learn from the other and in so doing would assist one another on their spiritual path.

I have heard Australian Aboriginal elders say essentially the same thing. One told me: "When the white people came, we welcomed them. We eagerly embraced their religion because we believed that the Christian church had some pieces of the secret that we did not have, and, if we all shared equally, everyone would be richer for it."

Then, with tears running down his cheeks, he continued, "It has taken us generations to see that their church does not have the secrets. We thought for generations that they had the secrets and just would not share them with us. Now we know that they just don't have them. We knew about Jesus long before they came."

I have heard this same story in different versions from Native people the world over.

How did our old ones know to pray for the white race, the black race, the yellow race, and themselves, the red race, and were doing so long before any contact was made with Europeans, Africans, or Asians?

Remember, as Franklin Kahn, a now-departed Navajo elder once said, "I don't care how a person prays. What I care about is that he does pray. Then, he is always welcome to stand beside me." To him and our old ones, differences were not a threat, they were an opportunity for more spiritual growth and knowledge.

I remember sitting and listening to my elders talk when I was a child. That was always one of my favorite activities, just sitting and listening to the old ones muse about what was really important. Grandma always said that this was an important, if not *the* most important, part of my education, so I sat with the elders a lot.

Sometimes they talked and sometimes they didn't. And, there was always something going on.

Often, those who knew one another well would say a few things, and then they would be quiet for long (what seemed to me long) stretches of silence. I would wait for an interminably long time, and then would pull on Grandma's dress and look at her imploringly. She would put her index finger over her mouth, shake her head no, and tell me to be quiet.

Later, we would "discuss" it.

"But Grandma," I would say, "they aren't *saying* anything. They aren't *doing* anything. They are just *sitting*. Sometimes it looks like they are sleeping."

"Oh, how foolish you are my granddaughter," she would say. "Have the patience to learn. They are communicating all the time. One does not always need words to communicate about the important things. You must learn to communicate and to listen on many levels, even when you 'hear' nothing. Have patience."

So, I would sit and "listen" with all my being, and soon I would "hear" them. Often, they did not use words about the most important matters for there are no words about what is most essential. Slowly, at my grandmother's knee, I learned to hear what people were saying when they weren't talking.

There was such support in my family to welcome and be open to any possible learning that was "different."

As I recounted earlier, when I was five years old in 1939, we decided that my father would leave his job in Fayetteville, Arkansas, and we would travel to California and try gold mining. We had a friend who was out on the Klamath River in Northern California, who had made friends with the Native people there, the Karuk Tribe, and wanted us to partner with him since my father had all the technical information and skill to invent a bigger rig for a better operation. So, off we went for the adventure of our lives. (I have written about this "adventure" in *Tales of the Klamath River*.)

Although we had traveled some, we had mostly stayed secure in our little Cherokee nest in Watts, Oklahoma, and were not really what one would call sophisticated or worldly people. So, this was a big deal, indeed.

One of the first people we met when we arrived on the Klamath River was "Frenchie." We knew white people, Indians, and black people, and had never met a Frenchman or anyone from a foreign country before. Instead of being guarded, suspicious, or cautious, my family was open and curious. He had been convicted of murder in a barroom fight in France. Of course, we knew (and he said) he was innocent. He had been sentenced to the French Foreign Legion and sent to Africa. After some time, he escaped and came to the Klamath River, working on ships as he made his way. He taught us about France, Africa, and the world out there. He still wore the large cummerbund sash/belt that he had worn as a Legionnaire and now served him as a back brace. He showed me how he fastened it to a bedpost and then wound himself up in it every day. He let me try it. We had never heard of lentils, and he taught my mother how to cook them. My parents treated him as family and very soon, I was sitting on his lap as he told us stories around the campfire. When we left the Klamath River, we left a French family member there.

To my parents, his different ways, his unusual (to us) accent, and his world perspective were not a threat to their views. They were secure in their worldview and believed that all different ways they encountered were opportunities for personal, emotional, and spiritual growth.

In the Native worldview, differences, even different religions, as I said, are all needed and seen as different pathways that we walk up the mountain to try to understand God. To the Native mind, it is inconceivable that we would try to destroy or annihilate other religions, spiritualities, or ways because all hold pieces that we need to get a fuller picture. To the Native being, it is quite astonishing that one would do anything but welcome differences as they offer such possibilities; to be threatened by differences must be some kind of joke.

This attitude of welcoming or needing differences to help complete our own wisdom and worldview makes the welcoming of the "newcomers" to this land more understandable.

Closed systems see differences as a threat. I have often said that the largest issue facing the planet today is how open systems can survive and stay open when the very core of a closed system is to destroy everything unlike itself. If there is an answer to this dilemma, I believe it is held in the Native worldview, and those seeds planted so long ago by our ancestors. It is creatively embedded in our ancient wisdom of valuing differences.

Participating in the Process of Valuing Differences

So how do we participate in the process of learning to value differences and not be threatened by them at our deepest levels?

First, we need to ask, "What are we afraid of?"

Are we so unsure of our worldview that we are fearful of letting any new ideas in?

I have seen some religions "homeschool" because they want to "indoctrinate" their children with their beliefs and do not want them exposed to any other worldviews at all. What is the basis of the fear?

Fear will almost always force us into being more and more controlling.

Are we willing to look at our fears and our urge to control and deal with them?

Children are naturally curious.

What has happened to *our* curiosity?

Our old ones were incurably curious and saw new knowledge as adding to their store of wisdom. When did the new and unfamiliar become a threat?

It is very Native to live out of being open and curious.

What's the problem?

The Eleventh Process

Being of Service

WE ARE HERE TO HEAL, learn, and be of service. Being of service is one of the major vehicles we have to heal and learn.

A life of service is so embedded in the Native way of being in the world that it is rarely articulated because it is always assumed. We all are given and have our own particular gifts and talents. There has never been a person born whom the Creator did not imbue with gifts and talents. Trying to homogenize ourselves and our children, or imposing our agendas and pathways on them, is an anathema to a Native person. It just is not done!

The Creator in infinite wisdom, much beyond what we humans are capable of, has imbued each being with pieces that are necessary for the healthy functioning of the whole. If a person is gay, different, or unusual, this is an indication of the creativity of the Creator and to be respected and appreciated. God does not make mistakes.

In the Native way of being, the role of parents and adults is to bring the unique characteristics of each individual forth so that that person can serve the Creator in a way that only that person can. To not support the unique creation of the Creator would be to reject the wisdom of the God who made us all.

It is as if the universe is one big puzzle, and everyone and everything in that universal puzzle has a place. When we don't develop our uniqueness and take our place in that big moving puzzle, the universe has a hole in it.

We have moved away from the path of developing our unique gifts and serving the Creator as best we can, and therefore we cannot take our place with our uniqueness and have come to a time when the universe has a lot of holes in it.

Some believe that it is time for the Native people to speak up about valuing differences and uniqueness so that we can maximize our unique gifts, honor them, and be of service as only we can be of service.

There is no one who was not born to be of service and no one who does not need to be of service with her or his unique gifts in order to be whole and contribute to the wholeness of all creation.

No matter who you are, you have unique gifts. No matter who you are, you need to be supported to develop those unique gifts. Thus serving the Creator.

Every tree, every rock, every animal, every blade of grass, and every person has a role to play in the spiritual growth in all of creation. It is much easier for the rocks, animals, and trees to play their role than it is for the human beings. We think too much and tend to try to impose our will and beliefs on our children. Trees and rocks don't do that. Therefore, we as humans have a special challenge to honor and respect every aspect of creation and, as best we can, develop our gifts and talents so we can become who we are meant to be and use our unique gifts to serve all creation.

One of my friends described to me the problems she was having in her life. She summed it up by saying, "I keep believing in the illusion of a personal life and feeling that I *should* have a personal life."

She went on to say that she believed in a personal life and that she should have what she wanted when she wanted it and be able to do what she wanted to do when she wanted to do it. She was seeing time and again that she was trying to live out of self-will and it was not going so well. At a very deep level, she was having trouble trusting that the Creator wanted something better for her and something better for all creation than she, herself, could possibly imagine.

She thought she was in charge! And it wasn't going so well.

Living a life of service means that we do everything we can do to heal and grow in the ways of the Creator.

If we are open, we will get a lot of information about how to live a life of service and contribute the talents we have been given to the greater whole.

It takes time and patience to be able to listen to and hear the voice of the Creator.

When I was a child, I was often told—especially when I did something wrong—"Look inside, Elizabeth Anne, didn't you feel uncomfortable? You *knew* you were doing something wrong, didn't you?"

There was always the understanding that "inside" if I would but listen, I would find the necessary information.

I longed for voices or irrefutable "signs" of what was the right thing to do, yet usually had to be satisfied with whispers, feelings, and "knowings" of what the Creator wanted from me.

Sometimes, quite often, in fact, I would make mistakes. Mistakes were always welcomed by my family—often with great laughter and teasing and a, "That's okay, Elizabeth Anne, you created a mess and mistakes are good. The Creator lets us make mistakes so we can learn. We are here to learn. The more we learn the better we serve."

As a child, I was surrounded by a family who knew that they were here to serve, and they served as best they could. They did not make a big deal out of serving. They did their serving out of humility—very quietly.

We accepted the people who came to our door to be healed just as we accepted the wounded and broken animals who appeared, needing to be healed. All were a part of God's creation and helping with healing others was my great-grandmother's job and my mother's job. They were very clear that *they* did not heal. Healing just happened as they opened to the healing powers of the Creator coming through them. The Creator healed. There was no confusion or dispute about that. Their way of serving was to be a conduit through which that healing power would flow. I don't believe they ever even considered taking credit for anything. It was the work of the Creator, and they only served.

I do not ever remember seeing or feeling or experiencing any piety or false piety related to the work my great-grandmother and mother did. The work was always done with a clear knowing that they were here to serve, and they were serving to the best of their ability.

It was easy. Life was easy. There were some economic issues and life always presented problems to be solved. At the same time, there was an infinite trust that if we just tried to do the work of the Creator as best as we understood it, we would always have all we needed—and more!

I am seventy-nine years old and, so far, that truth has always proven to be a reality in my life.

This reality does not mean that I do not have to work! I work very hard. In fact, I have learned not to trust people who don't work or are not willing to work. Working and serving are a big part of life as are resting, playing, and enjoying life.

It is not possible to be a spiritual person if you do not know how to work and serve. All of life is linked.

We have the responsibility to develop the gifts we have been given in our DNA and in our uniqueness and use those gifts to serve.

Participating in the Process of Service

Our heads can never tell us what to do in this life. Heads can rarely be trusted, nor should they be. Native people learned not to trust our thinking eons ago and, at the same time, learned to accept our minds, when used well, as a gift of the Creator.

Our minds are best used as a place to gather, store, and sort information that comes from various sources. Noticings, awarenesses, intuitions, inspirations, words of others, information from "knowings," and nature can be sorted by our thinking. And it is usually best when our thinking follows and does not lead.

When our lives are one of using our unique gifts to serve—without need for recognition—we just, quite simply, do better.

It's all so simple.

See what you can do to accept the gifts you were given, refrain from imposing your "thinking" on them, be grateful for them, and serve.

Service is the cornerstone to a fulfilling and good life.

Humility—true humility—helps. As we let our lives unfold and participate in it as fully as we can, we will "know" how to be of service. Opportunities are always just right in front of us.

Never impose your service on others. To serve is to make the world a better place in every way, every day for everyone.

We do not need to worry about another's service. Ours will keep us busy enough.

The Twelfth Process

Living in Our Bodies and Taking Care of Them

EVERY BODY IS BEAUTIFUL. Every body is a design of the Creator. And, there is something about taking care of and living out of and in the body that the Creator has given us while honoring it as a part of all creation that is very comforting and healing.

In the story I told about my great-grandmother bathing me and readying me for bed, every action, every movement, every process taught me to respect and honor my own body. She did not need to say anything. Her actions said it all.

Our bodies, too, are gifts from the Creator and should be treated as such—to value, respect, and honor.

In the Native way of thinking, we have the bodies we have for a reason. It is inconceivable that we would alter them for some abstract, temporary cultural notion of beauty. How can we improve on the work of the Creator? We may wish that we had inherited another body, and that's not the issue. When we honor the Creator (and our ancestors) we accept the body we have been given and take care of it as a part of creation. If we accept that we are to be of service to all creation, we accept that the Creator has given us the bodies we need to carry out the work we have been given to do. Our bodies are one of the vehicles we have been given to aid in our healing, growing, and learning. Our job is to care for them and accept and learn what we can from the bodies we have been given—and to enjoy them.

This does not mean that we as Native people have not abused our bodies—we certainly have. In our lost-ness and bewilderment in the world in which we find ourselves, we have lost our way as much as anyone. Yet, somewhere deep in the knowledge of our ancestral blood, we know better. We know our bodies are sacred and this knowledge only adds to the pain we feel for the abuse we have inflicted upon ourselves. Down deep, we know that when we do not honor and respect our bodies, we do not honor and respect our Creator.

We are not at the mercy of our bodies. We are here to live in and work with our bodies.

When I was a child, I would spend hours watching spiders weave their webs, bugs doing their work, chickens teaching their little ones to find food, and birds building their nests. Sometimes Grandma would sit with me. She would comment on the intricacy of the spider web, the absolute wonder of the knowledge that the spider had to build it and the fact that we as humans did not have the same skill. As she marveled at the knowledge and skill of the spider and the unique body the spider had to be able to accomplish the miraculous feat of building the spider web, she was also teaching and reminding me to notice how miraculous *my* body was and how capable it was to help me do the work *I* needed to do.

We marveled at my fingers and toes when I was quite little. I have clear memories of this. She rejoiced when I was able to handle more and more complex tasks as my body matured and grew. My family seemed to have a special sense that helped them to push me to my limits so I expanded and grew. Yet, they knew not to push me far beyond my limits so that I got in trouble with my body or learned not to trust it. In spite of their best efforts to help me expand my horizons and, at the same time, respect my limitations, my uncles and I sometimes did not listen and my body was damaged. I also had the opportunity to learn from these excursions.

"She really wanted to try it," my favorite playmate/uncle would plead on his own behalf.

"Yes," the elders would say. "But you are older and you should have more sense. She is just learning what her limits are."

With wonderful uncles as models, it was difficult to accept that my limits might be different from theirs. And, often, with older uncles, I frequently learned that my limits were not as constricting as my parents and grandparents believed. I was always testing my body, and it usually has responded with strength and agility.

I remember one time when I was about six or so and my uncle and I were playing Buck Rogers (one of the early "space men") under a tree. We both thought our space adventure would be more authentic if we were *in* the tree. It was a big sycamore. My uncle could climb it and I couldn't (a situation I hated).

After a long assessment of the situation, he decided that if we had a block and tackle, he could fix it up in the tree, and then he could pull me up, and we would have a much better Buck Rogers time. So, off we went to ask Grandpa where we could get a block and tackle.

Absentmindedly Grandpa responded, "Out in the shed."

Off we went happily eager for our new adventure. We were busily stringing up the device in the big old sycamore when Grandpa breathlessly appeared on the scene.

"What are you doing?" he panted.

"I'm fixing this up so I can pull Elizabeth Anne up in the tree. We're playing Buck Rogers," my uncle replied.

"Give me that!" Grandpa growled with more force than usual. "Are you crazy? Elizabeth Anne is too little to get up in that tree."

He grabbed the block and tackle and the rope and went off mumbling to himself.

Uncle Leslie and I waited, reconnoitered, and looked at other ways to launch me into space. We discovered there was one low limb that he could bend down if he carefully crawled out on it. Miraculously, I could reach the limb when he bent it down. Then, when he jumped off, I was flipped up in the tree, if I hung on tight.

We space travelers spent the rest of the day in that big sycamore tree and no one was the wiser. We did not feel the need to share our adventures in detail with the family because there were more to come.

I learned to be sensible and cautious with my body from my grandparents and risk-taking and adventurous with my body from my uncles. Both learnings have served me well. Part of growing up and respecting my body has been learning how to balance the need to push my body to its limits with the need to respect its limits and abilities. Thus I developed a relationship with my body that serves me to this day.

The whole world was a classroom to learn to live in, and with, my body.

Not to learn what it is capable of would have been disrespectful.

Not to accept its limitations would have been disrespectful. To live in it has been a great adventure.

All of these learnings have served me well in being in and with my body and honoring it through the different stages of my life and dealing with somewhat severe automobile and train accidents. We live well together, my body and I. I've had my difficulties, often due to eating foods that my Native body has not done well with. Still, we are really great friends.

Participating in the Process of Our Bodies

We will never get our bodies the way we want them and have them stay that way.

Our bodies are a process—one piece of the overall process we have been given by the Creator. We have the opportunity to accept, love, and care for them and try not to abuse them in any way. Respecting our bodies requires that we accept them and we honor what they can do and cannot do and the process of their changes.

If you have breasts and a vagina, you need to deal with that. If you have breasts and a vagina and do not feel like you should be a woman, you have to deal with that. Your uniqueness can be of service to the Creator.

We need not to impose false gods, idols, and ideas on our bodies.

How much time and energy it takes to want to or try to make our bodies different from what they are. Obsessing about our bodies leaves us less time to live and serve.

Caring for our bodies and accepting them for what they are is the Native way. We accept the material, we are not ruled by the material; there is more to us than what exists in the material plane.

Our bodies will tell us when we need to drink water, when we need to eat, and when we need to rest, if we listen and do not cloud these messages with our thinking.

The Thirteenth Process

Listening and Humor

No one listens like an Indian, and there is always something to laugh about when one has the advantage of a broad perspective of the universe.

Listening is a built-in skill for the Native person. When one respects and honors another person, one listens to them. When one respects and honors the animals and all creatures, one listens to them. When one respects and honors the swimming and the flying, one listens to them. When one respects and honors the plants, trees, and all of nature, one listens to them all. When one is familiar with and respectful of the unseen, one listens to the unseen also.

Listening is not only our responsibility, it is an honor and a gift to be able to listen to all that is around us, acknowledge its existence, and have the opportunity to learn, heal, and grow spiritually from all of it.

I have found that, often, people seem surprised that I actually listen to them. They are even more surprised that I like listening to them and, not unusually, frightened that I listen to them so carefully.

In exploring this curious phenomenon more thoroughly, I have discovered that few people really, really *listen*. They don't listen to their own insides, knowings, and intuitions. They don't listen to what they, themselves, are saying. And, they don't listen to what others are saying.

Having grown up in a family where everyone listened carefully, I am still shocked when I am not listened to or when others are surprised that I have listened to them.

Not listening is not only rude, it is stupid. No one ever said to me that when an elder is speaking to me, it is because I have something important to learn. I seem to have always known that.

I did hear mumblings about being shocked that people in the dominant culture did not listen to Native people and especially the elders. To my people, the brains of the old ones could not compute that anyone in their right mind would not listen to an elder. How could they risk not learning what was there to learn and what they needed to learn to live in a good way? What dire things could happen (and are happening!) if you did not listen to your cars, your homes, or to nature. My elders did not even want to consider the possibilities.

Listening is not merely a courtesy, it is essential for survival and spiritual growth.

I am often accused of having the ears of an elephant and being able to "hear" people that are miles and miles away. I do listen carefully to all the information that comes at me. It would be rude and disrespectful not to, and all of it is interesting and important. One never knows when a nugget will be buried in a ton of verbiage. This does not mean that I will let a person go on and on. When one is a "listener"—a *real* listener—one can tell when a person is not listening to herself or himself, and then it is not good to validate that process by listening. Of course, one must be very careful in making a choice not to listen and this choice should be done rarely and with great respect.

Years ago, in the early 1960s, I was working with a group of Black men to help train them to become facilitators for NTL (National Training Laboratory). After a few weeks of working with me, a delegation approached me.

"We need to talk," they said.

"Is there a problem?" I asked.

"Well . . ." they drew out the word slowly. "We have been talking about you, and we have decided you are a witch," they said cautiously.

I burst out laughing.

They were not so amused.

"Am I a bad witch or a good witch?" I asked trying not to smile.

"We're not sure. That's why we came to you," they continued.

"If you thought I was a bad witch, would you have come to me to talk about it?" I queried carefully.

Pause . . .

"Then we don't have a problem," I said softly.

More silence . . .

"Why do you think I am a witch?" I asked.

"Well, you seem to remember everything we say. You seem to know what we are thinking, what we are feeling. It's creepy," they responded.

"Are you afraid of me?" I asked.

More silence—then all shook their heads. "No."

"It's just creepy," one offered.

"Do you want to know what my secret is?" I asked.

All heads vigorously nodded affirmatively.

"I listen to you," I said matter-of-factly. "I listen to what you say and what you don't say. I listen to your words, your sounds, your gestures, and your unspokens.

"Listening this way is how my elders taught me to respect people. Are you not accustomed to being listened to?" I asked feeling sad.

Again, a pause . . . then . . .

"No, ma'am, we're not," said a brave one.

Long pause.

"Then we're really going to have some fun, aren't we?" I said teasing them. "Wait until you hear what I find out from you. Beware!" I teased further.

We all laughed together and relaxed. From that moment on we happily worked together, and they basked in being listened to and heard.

How often in my life have I heard that people feel nervous around me because they fear I can see through them and see things they don't even know about themselves!

I always reply, "What an opportunity! We all need to bring our blind spots into the light so that we can heal and grow and not be ruled by the unconscious—the unseen!"

Maybe this is where the myth of the "inscrutable Indian" came from. Maybe the discomfort the newcomers experienced came from the unfamiliar feeling of being listened to when they themselves had forgotten how to listen to themselves, or to others.

As I mentioned earlier, some of the old timers who knew one another well did not need many words to communicate. Progressively, their communicating and listening took place on another plane.

Good listening results in that kind of conversation.

I find that all too often people are incapable of listening because they have so much chatter going on in their heads that they don't have the time and energy left to listen to anyone else. To listen, we have to attend carefully and, simultaneously, calm our own chatter. Good listening combines many processes.

Our old ones knew that our world was colorful and multidimensional when we were able to listen to it. Speaking and seeing were skills that were greatly valued indeed. And, hearing and listening also ranked exceedingly high in the gifts to be cherished. There is so much information available to us when we can listen with all our being. The world takes on colors, hues, dimensions, and perspectives that are just not there if we are not able to listen carefully. One who listens like an Indian has a much richer world than someone who does not. Once when I first went to Australia, I spent all of my time with Aboriginal people who took me to meet various elders. One eighty-year-old elder we went out in the bush to meet had "gone walkabout." She was keeper of the women's sacred sites in that area and had duties to perform.

We heard she had gone east toward some possible towns and we headed in that direction. Often we would stop to listen. Usually a bunch of crows would gather and chatter away.

"The crows are our messengers," the elder woman said. "They are guiding us."

"I know," I said. "The crows are also our messengers. And, I don't speak Aboriginal." We all laughed.

Looking for her would have been like looking for a needle in a haystack, and, thanks to the crows, we drove right up to the house where she was.

I recently heard about an old Indian woman in Montana who lived in a traditional way. Every summer she moved to her summer camp. There were a lot of cattle around and she always took her cattle dog, J.D. (Just Dog), to keep the cattle out of camp. There were always white people coming into camp to "see Indians," which she didn't like too much. One day a woman slipped into camp and headed right for her. J.D. was sitting under her chair.

"Is that a dog?" said the woman.

"Yep," said the old Indian woman.

"But there's a sign that says, 'No dogs allowed.'"

The old woman paused. "Yep," she said . . . "But J.D. can't read."

There are many important uses for humor and good humor requires acute listening on many levels.

As the story is told, it seems that this white woman decided for herself that she was going to learn from this old Indian woman and rudely announced that she wanted to know where she could sleep. The old Indian woman, with a twinkle in her eye, called over a helper and said, "Show her down to that tent by the river."

"You mean the one where the bear goes by?" asked the helper.

"Yeah, that one," answered the elder.

So she was shown to the tent by the river, where she was to sleep.

The next morning the old Indian woman asked where "that white woman" was.

"She's gone," said the helper.

"Do you reckon that bear ate her?" the elder asked.

"I doubt it," said the helper. "Her car is gone too."

Humor can be used in many ways by Native people. And it is!

For humor to work well, one has to listen carefully.

There is a strong and almost magical link between listening and humor. Our Native ancestors had a lot of fun, and their lives were filled with humor, teasing, and laughter. No matter how poor and without material possessions Native people are, they can always tease, joke, and laugh at almost anything, themselves in particular. Often the Native humor and teasing are not understood by the dominant culture so Native people have learned to keep them under wraps when surrounded by others. Yet, when on their own, Native people giggle, laugh, and guffaw at almost anything.

They will take a situation that is sad, even horrible, and find humor in it. This ability is usually misunderstood by others. When a Native person is sharing about some really stupid thing she or he has done and the audience is just cracking up, others tend to see this behavior as disrespectful. A Native person—when those who are laughing are also Native—feels loved and understood.

I have continued to be astonished with the way people raised in the dominant culture respond to teasing.

In my family, teasing was multifaceted and multileveled and all good.

We were teased when we did something wrong. We were teased when we did something right. We were teased to bring us down to our right size when we got "too big for our britches" and teased when we refused to admit our gifts.

Teasing was always a major vehicle for learning. It was much more effective to be teased into awareness and learning than it was to be pushed by being disciplined or lectured to. We felt sorry for kids whose families did not know how to deliver learning through teasing. How could everyone enjoy learning if they didn't have teasing around?

It wasn't until I left home that I ever even considered that teasing could be used in a bad or harmful way. I found it almost unbelievable that any family used teasing to shame, put down, or hurt. These uses were just not in any repertoire I had ever experienced.

I was shocked when I encountered people who did not enjoy being teased. How could that be?

When I learned that there were people who came from families who used teasing to harm, tears rolled down my cheeks. How could something that is so good and so much fun be used in a bad way? I didn't understand. It did not seem possible to me that teasing could be used for punishment or humiliation. I just could not relate.

"I only tease people I love," I would say. "Teasing you means that I am taking the time and energy to give you special loving and—there may be the possibility for a learning to be embedded in it too." Teasing can be very rich indeed. Not to tease people I love would be like having a limb missing. It's like cutting off a love conduit. It hurts, and one loses so much fun, joy, and learning in the process.

Why would anyone not tease?

Clearly Native people have many forms of humor that are not understood by everyone.

We enjoy them anyway.

Participating in the Process of Listening and Humor

Humor, good humor, requires a great deal of careful listening. Not only must the perception be loving, creative, and fun, the timing has to be just right for it to be effective. Listening with one's whole being helps develop the skill to see the humor in oneself, others, and our universe.

Both the ability to listen and a good sense of humor are gifts to be fed and treasured. I believe that these two gifts are present in everyone. In some they have just been buried deeper than in others.

Garrison Keeler has quite effectively proven that even the Scandinavians can be funny . . . which gives hope for us all. (That was a teasing joke—not to be confused with a jab. The energy is different.)

For those who have lost their listening skills and their humor—these can be regained. It just takes practice. Expect to be rusty at first. When listening and humor are regained, your world will take on more colors and dimensions—I think!

Try it! You'll like it!

A people who lose their humor and ability to laugh are a lost people indeed.

The Fourteenth Process

Living in Context—Don't Waste, Don't Abuse

THE WORLD OF THE NATIVE PERSON is expansive and emerges from wholeness.

Part of being Native is to recognize and understand that we can only LIVE in context. Rugged individualism is an unsubstantiated myth perpetuated more by fantasy than reality. Making it on your own, not ever needing anyone or relating to anything other than yourself is an illusion. It is just not possible. We can only live in context, recognizing that we influence everything around us (and beyond) and are influenced by everything around us. How can we ignore the reality of our family, our community, our society, or our planet? We all live in context, no matter who we are or where we are. Being self-centered may be the norm for the culture in which we live, and it is not the reality for the culture in which we live.

Since we *can* only live in context, admitting that we do live in context makes our lives more flowing.

Native people have recognized for centuries that what we do affects everything around us and is affected by everything around us. Our old ones were aware that bugs were important to maintain the balance, and they needed to care for the bugs like they cared for the land or none of them would survive. They were aware that a delicate balance existed throughout all creation and we, as humans, had a great responsibility to maintain that balance.

To live in context means that we are aware of our surroundings. Living in context means that we consider that context in all that we do.

For example, if we are waiting to be taken care of in a store, a traditional Native person will be aware of her/his context. A traditional Native person will be very aware of who came when and who is next and will never try to break the queue to get ahead of someone whose turn is first. Living in context, a traditional Native person will also always step aside for an elder, regardless of when they joined the line, because they live in context and live out of being Native. They will also always be a little shocked and surprised (even to this day) when others do not understand and live out of these respectful ways of living in context. After hundreds of years, Native people still are shocked when others do not know how "decent people" behave.

Living in context means being considerate of others in all our doings.

When I was a child, sleep was sacred in our household. When anyone was sleeping, we all were aware of it and did not talk in loud voices, make loud noises, or turn on the radio. As a very young child, I learned to be aware of my surroundings and live within my surroundings. I never felt that I was being deprived when someone was sleeping and I needed to be quiet. I felt that I was a part of something bigger than myself and knew that I would get the same consideration. As I look back, I see that this "living in context" developed a kind of security in me that exists to this day.

I feel so sad when I see children being raised like they are the center of the universe and the entire world revolves around them. They end up being anything but secure and have a terrible burden placed upon them before they have any skills to cope with that burden. People raised as if they do not live in context end up being insecure, self-centered, angry, unhappy, and lonely. It is sad to see. Their parents, in trying to do what they think is the right thing, have handicapped them, teaching them to live a very constricted life on this planet.

As my old ones would say, "It's not the child's fault. Their parents did not teach them the right way to live."

Living in context requires a great deal of watching, waiting, and listening, resulting in a kind of patience with oneself and the universe. This is because, in order to live in context, one has to be aware of context. One of the reasons our old ones were so "inscrutable" was that they were always trying to size up situations that made no sense to them whatsoever. They found themselves in a context that mocked and defied everything they had been taught about the world, as well as all their spiritual teachings. No wonder Native youth have become angry and lost. No wonder, for some, alcohol has become the only solution. The conflict between their innate sense of "rightness" and the lack of that sense in their context is enough to drive anyone to drink. Getting back to the traditions, living in context, indicates a way back to the reality we "know" in our DNA.

Living in context is a way to affirm with our lives that we know that we are a part of that living, pulsing web which is all of creation. *Not* to be aware of our surroundings and *not* to respond to, care for, and relate within that context is self-defeating and stressful indeed.

Most of all, ignoring that we live in context is lonely. It is a loneliness of the soul that can only be solved by the way we live out our lives, participating as best we can within our context and being aware of it, no matter where we are.

I have been told by Native people the world over that (of all the Europeans) the Irish are the closest to Native people. It is written about the Irish that when they traveled—and they traveled a lot—they never tried to colonize like other Western European nations. When they came to another country, they assimilated and learned the ways of the people there. No wonder the Irish are thought to be more like them by Native people the world over. They know about living in context and are respectful of context, which is essential to being Native.

As our little worlds expand, we are called upon to live in larger and larger contexts. An isolated little house in the suburbs will no longer suffice to raise children to live in larger and larger contexts (if it ever did). We need to rediscover and expand our skills for living in context.

Living in context may mean that we have to give up some of our personal "toys" and indulgences. The rewards and survival implications for learning to live in context are, however, crucial if we are to survive as a planet and a species. For example, why does every house in every suburban neighborhood need a lawnmower when one would suffice for the whole neighborhood? Living in context is, indeed, necessary for survival of the planet.

Participating in the Process of Living in Context

Our old ones always knew that hunting together was better than hunting alone . . . that living in community was better than living alone . . . that living in context was the only way to live serenely.

Start practicing little ways of being aware of and living in context.

Be aware that you can have and need to have a relationship with your home, your cars, and your community.

Begin to notice what decisions you make that deny that you live in context and see how you feel when you make those decisions.

Nurture your Native soul by finding more and more ways to live in context.

Ask for help from your ancestors if you need it.

Living in context means not wasting—not abusing our world around us.

The Fifteenth Process

Science

THE WORLD OF THE NATIVE PERSON is expansive and emerges from and returns to wholeness.

Before we begin to explore the world of Native science, we need to clear up some popular misconceptions.

First of all, there is not just one science. In the dominant culture, when the word *science* is used, the assumption is that so-called Western science is "the" science, and whenever one talks about science, one, by default, is talking about Western science. This assumption just is not true.

For example, we find Chinese science, Japanese science, Australian Aboriginal science, Western science, Mayan science, and, for our purposes, Native American science to name a few. Although all Native sciences have more in common than not, the specifics of the content may change from culture to culture and the assumptions, processes, and roles of all Native sciences have much in common.

It is important to remember that there is no one science, no one set of thinking processes that define the "true" science, and no one form or methodology that is the only one true approach to "science" and discerning "reality" or "truth." There may be elements in common and, like religions, every approach may have a piece of the "truth" in finding out more about our world and none is "the only way." In the Native world, to believe one has the *only* way is a serious problem indeed.

In general, the role of science is to help us observe and understand our world. In Native science, we do not seek to predict and therefore control our world, we seek to learn to live with, more fully interact with, and participate with all aspects of our world so as to create an expanding wholeness as we care for all creation. Native science is about understanding, acceptance, and living with. We will predict to "live with" in a better way. At the same time, predicting in order to control the natural world is not part of the Native psyche. Native science is about noticing, wonder, and gratitude.

Native science does not limit itself to the seen or what can be observed and measured. Native science is, indeed, concerned with observation and it will also, sometimes, measure. Yet, the purpose of the observation and measuring is not for the purpose of prediction and control. In Native science, the focus is upon living with, serving, and caring for all aspects of the universe—not just the humans.

Native scientists often ask for and get help from the spirits, and this "data" is valued as much or more than that observed with the senses. Native scientists are those who check with and know the seen and unseen and attempt to grasp the meaning of it all. Native scientists listen to the subtle and the quiet as well as the obvious. To observe clearly, one must weed out the influence of the unconscious, personal biases, and assumptions, and be a "hollow bone" for as much information to come through and be processed as possible.

For example, on Fajada Butte in Chaco Canyon in Northern New Mexico, there is one of the most accurate sun and moon calendars in the world. It is awe inspiring to learn about this calendar when one realizes that the moon has an eighteen-year cycle. This fact alone suggests a very sophisticated observation and measuring ability that can be respected by any of the world's approaches to science.

So what is science, then? Science, quite simply, can, in its broadest sense, be understood as a way to try to understand and live with our world.

In general, Western science, by definition, limits itself to measuring, predicting, and controlling the material plane that are integrated with and, in many aspects, help define a culture and the way it thinks and functions.

Native science includes the observation and study of the material plane (the seen) and it also includes the study and understanding of the unseen in order to participate in the wholeness of our reality. In Native science, there is no fear of the unseen, or the need to eliminate, ignore, or deny it. In Native science, there is an acceptance of the unseen as part of our reality. And, it is necessary to understand all of our reality in its wholeness so that we can better participate with and serve all creation.

Native science goes from the particular to the context to the whole and back again, recognizing that all aspects of creation are important and to be honored.

Rueben Kelly, an Australian Aboriginal elder who has since passed on, once said to me: "You white folks centuries ago decided to go the way of science and technology"—he was talking about Western science, I have found that most of us Native people at some level have bought the illusion that science and Western science are synonymous!—"and they will destroy the planet. We hope you figure this out before it's too late."

You can't fix the problem with the problem. He went on to say, "It is not that science and technology are necessarily bad. The problem is that Western culture has not grown enough spiritually to be able to develop a science and technology [recognizing there are many sciences] that would not be harmful to the planet."

Imagine a science and technology that is completely integrated into the wholeness and honors the Creator and all creation—the seen and the unseen!

Mr. Kelly continued to say, "We could have developed a science and a technology. We had the intelligence and all the resources we needed here in this great land, but we knew that we needed to evolve more spiritually in order to participate in the right kind of science. So we focused on our spiritual development. When the white people came, we had hoped to work together with each group adding its wisdom."

Sadly, this cooperation did not happen.

Imagine, if you can, a science that takes into consideration all creation and wants to participate fully and respectfully with all of it!

So, as we have a clear understanding that there are many "sciences," let us focus on the important elements of a Native science.

When I was a child, both my parents and those around me supported and encouraged open-mindedness. I was taught to observe—very, very carefully to observe. Watching, listening, observing, "waiting with" were all part of my early training.

"Keep your eyes and ears open and your mouth shut," was a mantra of my early childhood.

Questions were not discouraged actively. At the same time, it was clear that questions were only to be asked after I had done my own footwork of watching, listening, and observing.

At dinner, there were often discussions of "What did you see today, Elizabeth Anne?" I was always given time to report my "findings." Whether my findings were the observations of an insect at work or of the lightning in the afternoon thunderstorms, or the taste of the food, my reports were always a time of curiosity, fascination, hilarity, and, "Very good, very good!"

At an early age, I learned a curiosity about everything in creation that is still with me seventy-nine years later. In my scientific worldview, there is so much to learn that I will have enough to keep me busy all of my life and then some. I have eagerly studied advanced math, physics, much, much chemistry, biology, zoology, comparative anatomy (I loved that course—it was the only one that remotely allowed the awareness of the *process* of what we were studying), bacteriology (need I say more?), and have respected the limited worldview and methodology of Western science. Yet, I have really never received that respect for *my* science in return. That has been painful for me at times and now that I have a larger perspective, I, at least, understand why.

My father was the "scientist" of our family because he knew and understood Western science. I now realize that my mother was as much of a "scientist" in the Native science, because she was as observant and open-minded and recorded her observations in the form of creative writing, poetry, cooking, and healing.

For both my parents, open-mindedness was basic to living. My father actively taught me that open-mindedness was a key to every scientific endeavor. One simply must approach everything (taught by my father) and everyone (taught by my mother) with an open mind. Not only was it rude to have preconceived notions about anything or anyone, it was completely unproductive. Only when one had an open mind could one truly be in a position to learn.

If I wrote a thousand pages on open-mindedness, I would still never be able fully to express how crucial, basic, and valuable open-mindedness is to the Native scientist. Open-mindedness was so valued in my family that it was clearly a spiritual basis for learning. Not to be open-minded was an attack on the Creator. I simply cannot know all about a thing or a person and should never approach them with the assumption that I do.

My mother always said to me, "Don't judge a person because of the way she or he acts. We never know why a person acts a certain way and there are always reasons for the way they act. Try to look behind the behavior to understand. Never judge. Judging never helps with understanding."

Being open-minded meant that everyone and everything needed to be approached with respect and reverence. Whatever "it" was, it was not there just for my convenience, use, or comfort. "It" was a gift of the Creator and to be understood in that way. Because it was a gift of the Creator it was to be honored.

When I went to college, one of the major shocks I experienced was that the majority of "scientists" I encountered were not open-minded. The more famous ones, and the ones I liked the best, were not interested in protecting their territory, proving and reproving their hypotheses, or, in general, what I would now call being very "small-minded." Many others, however—the majority—were the antithesis of what I had been taught being a scientist meant. This shocking reality was painful for me to see and experience as I had so loved the "science" I had known and experienced up to that point. It has taken me years to realize that what I thought of as science and believed in was much larger, more open, and more inclusive than most of the science that was being presented to me as *the* "science." I now have more compassion and understanding, and, like Mr. Kelly, I now see the limitations of Western science and how broad and sophisticated is the science I was taught as a child.

I remember one time when I was speaking at an addictions conference in Moscow, Russia. I was presenting material from my book *When Society Becomes an Addict* in which I observed and postulated that Western culture exhibited the very same characteristics and patterns (especially thinking patterns) as an active alcoholic. Another "scientist," whose work focused on changes in brain chemistry, kept interrupting me and saying that my work was not scientific. I kept responding that it was, indeed, and went on.

Finally, I became exasperated and said that I could understand where he was coming from, and the science I espoused was not limited to reductionism nor did it use the same scientific methodology he used. My approach to science was broad and encompassed the totality of reality as we can comprehend it. I respected his reductionist approach as one way to glean a certain kind of data. Why could he not respect my eagle-eye view? Both and more were needed. He was completely perplexed with me, and, in the true fashion of his scientific belief system, needed to deny, discount, and dismiss anything that his science could not handle.

I had observed over the years that the majority culture assumes and believes that it knows and understands everything, and that if there is something it does not know and understand or cannot know and understand with its methodology of the "scientific method," then that "science" simply proclaims that the other reality simply does not exist. Any other reality has to be dismissed because it cannot be understood by the procedures of that limited science. I have seen every minority's knowledge and belief system dismissed in this way. No open-mindedness here. And, the reality is that Native people know and understand more because, in order to survive, we have to understand our own system (which, no matter how deep, is buried inside us) and the Western system as well in order to survive within it.

I had no trouble learning all the science and math I could in high school and college; and deep within, I knew there was more.

Open-mindedness had helped me accept, study, and enjoy all the science that was presented to me *and* that which was deep inside me. Because of my early teachings, I knew there was more to science than I was being taught in classes. This knowledge was painful at times, and it did see me through the hard times.

Another aspect of open-mindedness, or lack thereof, relates to the concept of objectivity. Native science does not accept "objectivity" as detachment, nonparticipation, and isolation. In fact, Native science knows that this kind of "objectivity" is not possible. Native scientists know that they are always one with and, by necessity, a part of that which they observe. Native scientists hope to reach a state of being in which they are clear enough inside not to impose their assumptions, biases, limitations, and unconscious interpretation on what they want to learn. This inner clarity is the Native form of objectivity and is achieved through hard work, many discussions with the Creator, humility, and open-mindedness.

In order to "understand" something, Western science generally takes whatever it wants to understand out of its context and reduces it to its most basic elements. This can be interesting and, it is just not enough.

Native science may, at times, be reductionistic, and in addition, it observes whatever it is observing in context, observes its context, and returns to and sees its place in the whole. *And,* all this is done while also seeing and respecting its process and that it—whatever "it" is—*is* a process to be respected as part of the whole of creation—the seen and the unseen. Native science is pretty neat that way.

As an extreme example—Western science, in order to understand the essence of "cat" would kill the cat and dissect it, reducing it to its most elemental elements and chemistry.

Native science might find that interesting. Yet, Native science is much more interested in the live cat in its context (why kill a cat—a creation of God for no reason?). What does the cat do? How does it relate to the rest of creation? What does it contribute to the whole of creation? How can it be honored as part of and necessary to the greater whole? And, what are the spiritual implications of "cat"? This is the greatness of Native science. The spiritual (not religious) is, by necessity, always included in what we think of as "science." Remember how differences were discussed as an opportunity, not a threat, in the Native mind? The Native worldview values differences. This worldview evidences itself in the way Native people "do" science.

Native people have no confusion about science *being* their worldview.

There are certain kinds of dominant-culture thinking that go along with Western science and that are not so prized or integrated into Native cultures, if they exist at all. I will discuss these more thoroughly in the next process. It is important to mention them here and to look at the ways they support a reductionistic science. They are dualistic thinking, contrast and comparison, hypotheses, constructs, and concepts. These approaches work to support the Western approach to science and, at the same time, limit the ability of our minds to move toward wholeness. Native people often are perplexed by disembodied concepts and constructs—not because they can't understand them—they can. They are perplexed as to why a worldview would want to proliferate and live in abstracts created by humans when the real world is so much more interesting and meaningful.

Native science is not and has never been or wished to become a religion or worldview.

In Native science, scientists are those who study the stars, the planets, the sun, and the moon to learn and accept their paths and stories. There is no need to try to control them. The Creator has created them, and our job is to participate with them, relate to them, and rejoice in their being. That's easy.

Native scientists are those who hear the unheard, see the unseen, know the unknowable, and respect the vastness and mystery beyond our knowing.

Native scientists are those who humbly ask the planets and animals to teach them the subtleties of healing, the beauty of taste, and the warning signs of things to come. The plants and animals can warn us of an oncoming hard winter or an especially dry summer ahead.

My mother knew a lot about horses and often knew what they were "saying" to us to try to help us. She would say, "The horses are getting an especially heavy coat for winter. It's going to be a cold one. We better be prepared." She was always right.

My grandmother was way ahead of the weathermen with predicting the weather—and much more accurate!

When I was first in Australia, I spent all my time with Aboriginal elders who had invited me to visit. I was taken "out in the bush" to see Aunt Millie, who was the keeper of sacred sights for the women in that area. I heard my first bellbird on that trip to find Aunt Millie. I will never forget that sound and the purity of it. I carry it with me in my being.

As I mentioned earlier, we were led to her by paying attention to the crows. These people were, rightfully, testing me every step of the way. Finally we found Aunt Millie. She was an old one and a sharp one. When she found out I was American Indian, she wanted to take me to White Buffalo Mountain. I, of course, agreed. When an elder wants to take you somewhere, you go!

Aunt Millie explained that this mountain had been an important one for some time. When the white people first came, the Aboriginals saw their cattle and called it White Bull Mountain. Then, when they learned about my people, they renamed it White Buffalo Mountain, because they knew that it belonged to my people and that it was a place my people came to rest after they died, before they moved on.

Intuitively, I knew this was a big test, and my white-trained mind got nervous. What if I didn't see what I should see? Maybe I was just a phony. It was too much of an honor to be shown this mountain. What if I failed? What if I weren't worthy to be representing my people? (Another attack of self-centeredness!)

I had a few bad moments there and then turned the whole process over to the Creator knowing that the process was in good hands and the outcome would be as it should be. When I first looked at the mountain—I saw a mountain. Then, after turning it all over to the Creator, what I saw was in the Creator's hands. With no warning, I suddenly saw a white buffalo charging out of the mountain right at me. Reflexively I jumped back, even though the mountain was miles away.

Aunt Millie smiled and nodded knowingly. "Uhhum!" she said.

"Uhhum," I said.

Our white drivers couldn't see it and wanted to know exactly what I saw where. They wanted me to describe it thoroughly. Their minds would not let them see it. Their science would not let them see it.

My Native science was fine with a white buffalo coming out of the mountain.

Aunt Millie said Fools Crow would be resting there soon.

As I said earlier, Western science can really only deal effectively with the static. It makes things static (like dissecting the cat) to study them. Native science is more comfortable with processes. It is about processes. It will study the static while knowing that stasis is an illusion and the process is what is important. Studying the process results in true open-mindedness because one never knows what a process will bring and must be open to whatever. Some call it chaos. Native scientists view it as a fascinating process of the universe encompassing more than humans on a material plane can ever understand. Because of this, Native science demonstrates a lack of attachment to hypotheses. Hypotheses are a bit cumbersome and might limit our open-mindedness if we aren't careful. In Native science, the process determines the order and organization, not the scientist. Order and organization are not artificially imposed upon nature.

I keep remembering my father's words to me: "The basis of science is open-mindedness, Elizabeth Anne. Keep your mind open to what you see. Don't think you see what you don't see. Don't decide what you are going to see before you see it."

With his support, I learned to "see" carefully, trust my perceptions, and always be open to test them. I needed to ask the spirits to help me see clearly. We always need help to fight off bias and "see" clearly. Open-mindedness helps.

Participating in the Process of Being in Native Science

We need to see and respect that, as Native people, we have a very advanced and sophisticated science. This is a science that is holistic, inclusive, respects the seen and the unseen, and is based on process.

There are many sciences. Native science is neither better than nor inferior to any other form of science. Native science is just different. Different is not a threat.

We need to practice open-mindedness. As Native people, open-mindedness is our spiritual birthright. We may feel, at times, that we have to protect ourselves by clinging tightly to what we think we know, and who we think we are. That process of static rigidity and closed-mindedness will harm us greatly and interfere with our *being* what we have to offer as Native people.

The possibilities are limitless for what our Native science can offer in understanding, participating with, and caring for all creation.

For example, a Native science would tell us that it is quite possible that our DNA can carry spiritual, psychological, emotional information and the wisdom from our ancestors, in addition to our physical genetics.

If we aren't so stuck with adherence to the physical plane, our information can be disembodied as well as embodied.

Native science can handle a wide range of possibilities to lead us toward more wisdom. Let's honor our ancestors and not limit ourselves.

We need to check to see if we have let Western science become a religion or worldview, and if so, see the limitations of that perspective.

Native science is inseparable from our spirituality and is an outgrowth of our spiritual nature. We need to be open to developing a science and technology that emerges from our spiritual wholeness.

Returning to Native science is *key* to our being Native.

The Sixteenth Process

Thinking

WHAT WE THINK is indeed important to us as Native people. Yet, the process of the way we think is even more important to understand if we hope to return to the wisdom of our ancestors. Native thinking is a very broad and complex process about which the dominant culture has little or no understanding.

In my experience, the actual content of what goes through a Native mind certainly has aspects that are uniquely Native.

As Lydia Whirlwind Soldier says in *Native Heritage*:

> We must be careful the public schools do not use our language to teach concepts that contradict our Lakota values. For example, the traditional concepts of cooperation over competition, generosity and compassion over materialism must be maintained. The desires of the individual ego over the welfare of the tribe is against our philosophy.*

Our language and our thinking are inextricably intertwined, as are our thinking and our scientific worldview. All the influences on our thinking and all aspects of Native thinking (and the thinking of the dominant culture!) would hardly be contained in one book. And, I do want to say something about the content and the process of Native thinking.

Native people do think about some of the same things that others do . . . food, relationships, debts, money, children . . . the usual. And,

---

* Arlene Hirschfelder, ed., *Native Heritage* (New York: Macmillan, 1995), 85.

we approach our thinking in a unique way. We spend a significant part of our thinking time clearing our thinking so we will be available for service, cooperation, generosity, compassion, and new information. That is what being a hollow bone means. For example, when a Native person goes to a garage sale, she does not just shop for herself—she thinks of family members, friends, someone she just met who would like this particular item. Her family is all creation and everything in it, and all are considered when the Native person is on a garage sale spree.

All Native people love garage sales, where we can have fun meeting people, talking and visiting (which Native people love). Bargains are thrilling to us, and we appreciate recycling (a service to the planet). It is not unusual for a Native person who has gone to a garage sale to come home with armloads of treasures, none of which are for herself. Her world is included in everything she does.

Native people think about science, philosophy, and business, yet these thoughts are almost always grounded in the present and what is real. When Native people talk about ghosts, spirits, animal conversations, or how the trees, wind, and rivers bring messages, they are talking about actual experiences not abstract, disembodied fantasies. The distinction between fantasy and a vast reality was clear to our ancestors. For example, Cochise, a leader of the Apache, said, "I was going around the world with the clouds when God spoke to my thought and told me to be at peace with all."

Cochise made a distinction as to what his thoughts were doing and the reality of the voice of God. One listens to the voice of God.

Native people know how easy it is to distort our thinking and convince ourselves of the reality of our distorted thinking.

Phil Lane Sr., the great Yankton Sioux spiritual leader, once said, "Don't trust the decisions you make with your head. The ones we make with our heart are more reliable."

Lee Piper, Tsa La Gi elder, once told me to be careful with my think-ing. "We can think ourselves into anything," she said. "We just can't trust our thinking."

It is not that Native people have such different thoughts. It is just that Native people seem to have a kind of realism about what our brains can do and what they can't. Native people seem to have a clear knowing that our thoughts and even our perceptions can be altered and distorted by our thinking, our wishes, our state of mind. In short, Native people do not worship their thinking and believe it is reality.

Native people do not build their reality out of abstractions and concepts. Concepts actually seem to stop our thinking process and our participation in our own process of living.

For example, many Native children have been told that they are dumb because they do not think in static, concrete thoughts. When the concept "dumb" becomes fixed in one's mind, the process of thinking stops and the static, fixed concept takes over one's thinking.

This same process happens in interpretations. A person may be angry with her father. This feeling becomes the static "fact"—"You hate your father." What may have started as a passing feeling gets concretized into "Why do you hate your father?" and that then becomes, "Your father abused you," and the "hating" is rationalized, justified, and concretized—with pain and alienation for all.

A Native person might take the same information, feel and process the resentment, anger, pain, and hurt, move through the healing that is nec-essary, have compassion for the father and all who have made mistakes, and trust the Creator that can heal all things and experiences. She would then see those experiences as part of her life experiences. She would see what she needs to do to heal and grow from these experiences and move on with her life and move toward wholeness.

To the Native person, the concept does not have the same weight it has in the Western world. Concepts and interpretations often have the effect of stopping the healing and/or living process and people stay stuck with their fixed idea.

I have a friend who has started to interpret his feelings of sadness and depression as, "I don't want to live." The feelings of sadness are real, present, and there. In truth, he doesn't really know what they are about at all. As soon as he interpreted the feeling to "mean" that he didn't want to live, he became stuck with that interpretation. Interpretations are nothing more than thoughts that have become concretized and then result in a mental constipation.

I once heard a friend of mine, a Seneca, say, "When we concretize our perceptions, we are participating in theological idolatry." Concepts are concretized perceptions that have lost the elasticity of process.

Interpretation is abusive when we do it to ourselves and when we do it to others. Interpretations tend to interfere with or stop the natural healing process and are almost always destructive. Interpretations are not natural for Native people.

Interpretations are like our "thoughts going around the world with the clouds." For Native people, our thoughts going around the world with the clouds is just fine—even good and necessary. The problem comes when we make our thoughts static and believe them. This is not the Native way.

Native thinking does not usually start with the brain. We do not start with abstract concepts or with thinking. We get feelings from our bodies, awarenesses, hunches, intuitions, knowings, flashes, and many other forms of information from the unseen and the seen, and then we take these to our brains for processing. Then we go back again to our "sources." Thinking is not linear or static for a Native person. Thinking and its content are a process.

Information comes to the Native person in many forms. Many of the teaching stories we were told as children focused on the trouble one could get into with thinking.

Old Brother Bear

Old Brother Bear sure wanted some of that honey the bees had made. He thought and thought about how good it would taste. The more he thought about it the more he wanted it. The more he wanted it, the more desperate he became. Lots of animals wanted some of that sweet honey, there was no doubt about that. But old Mr. Bear, here, he really, really wanted it, if you know what I mean.

Mr. Bear, he watched those bees come and go. He tried to figure a time when those bees all left the hive but they always kept a guard. He pretended to sleep nearby, but Turtle noticed that he always kept one eye half open toward the beehive. That old Mr. Bear, he got grumpier and grumpier as he thought about that honey and waited for the right time.

The other animals watched old Mr. Bear thinking about that honey, thinking about that honey, plotting how to get that honey, and plotting how to get that honey. They knew that there were other kinds of sweet things to get in the forest like berries, sassafras roots, or sweet hickory nuts so they went around having a good time putting up things for the winter and feasting in the forest.

That old Mr. Bear, he became so fixated on that hive of honey that he plumb forgot to start getting fattened up for the winter. He became so agitated about that honey that none of his friends could get near him to have some chat about winter coming and the weather changing and such things.

The bees were ready for him. There was no one in the forest who hadn't seen him thinking and plotting about that honey. Even the bees had heard the other animals gossiping.

"That old Mr. Bear, he has his mind so fixed on that honey that he's not even getting ready for winter."

"Too much thinking, I'd say," said the Blue Jay. "We have to leave soon and usually by the time we leave he's pretty fixed for winter, but not this year."

Everyone in the forest but Mr. Bear could see the kind of trouble his thinking was getting him into.

Finally, he had worked himself into such a frenzy with his thinking about that honey that he charged that tree and tried to grab the honeycomb.

The bees were ready for him. The foot soldiers crawled over him and stung him wherever they could. The queen's guard, the flying specialists, dive-bombed him and stung his eyes, around his mouth, his gums, and some even were willing to attack his tongue. It was a fierce battle.

Mr. Bear grabbed a little bit of a honeycomb but he was blind from the bee stings and his mouth and paws hurt so bad that he fell out of the tree and hit the ground with a huge thud and was knocked out for sure.

The other animals cautiously gathered around. They loved Mr. Bear and knew that he was part of their family. Yet, no one wanted to be around Mr. Bear when he was hurt or angry. So they just got into a big circle and waited.

He was so knocked out that Bobcat cautiously tried to lick his eyes a bit to heal them.

Turtle slowly went to the creek and brought back some mud, and raccoon patted it on his eyes as a poultice to soothe the bee stings. Even the bees brought little bits of honey and the ants crawled into his mouth and deposited it on his stings, for they all knew that honey was good for healing stings too.

Most of the animals took a taste of the sweet honey that was scattered on the ground or in Mr. Bear's fur, for every one of them liked that sweet honey but only Mr. Bear seemed greedy with it. The others seemed satisfied with what the bees dropped for them and the sweetness the flowers offered up before the bees got there. There was plenty to go around.

The dragonflies whispered to one another that it was a shame that Mr. Bear had thought and thought so much about that honey. They figured that all that thinking had made him a little crazy in the head.

The dragonflies buzzed around and talked with the other creatures of the forest, and they all agreed that they felt sorry for Mr. Bear and could see that all that thinking had sure enough caused great trouble for Mr. Bear.

They all agreed that they all like Mr. Bear really and that he just lost himself when he thought too much about that honey.

Mr. and Mrs. Porcupine agreed to guard the honeycomb so he would have it when he woke up. The bees agreed that they thought he had learned his lesson and they could work harder and make more honey before winter. Some of the other animals agreed to gather extra food and share some of their winter stores with Bear. They knew that when he woke up he would have a terrible headache with all that thinking and he was sure to be hungry.

All of the animals of the forest agreed to take part of that day and try to help Mr. Bear. Anyone could get silly sometimes and it was a good reminder of the kind of trouble that too much thinking could cause an otherwise good person.

All were happy that Mr. Bear was just knocked out and not dead.
They really liked him after all.

My great-grandmother told me many stories that revolved around the dangers of thinking. Our old ones had observed a lot of thinking in the white people.

There are many thinking processes that are just plain dangerous.

Western science is based on dualistic thinking. Dualistic thinking insists that things be either this or that. The world gets categorized and put in a this or that setup. These dualisms are static. They set up an either/or judgment. They are disembodied concepts. They simplify a very complex world into two choices and are always oversimplifications of reality, setting up choices where neither alternative is wanted or satisfactory.

Dualisms are very confusing to the Native thinking process as we realize that our world is multivariate and in process. Dualisms try to simplify a living process of a world and are artificial.

Native people don't like dualisms and feel trapped when caught in them, even though we may have incorporated them into our thinking process. For us, dualisms are unnatural and uncomfortable.

Much of Western science is based on dualistic thinking, and it limits a complex universe of process into either/or.

Comparisons are foreign to Native thinking as well. When one respects differences, why would a Native woman compare herself to another Native woman? The Creator has given each the gifts she has and it is up to each to develop these gifts as fully as possible. We are all here to honor the Creator and be of service. Contrast and comparison have no meaning in such a world. Native people have seen how much trouble comparison and contrast have caused in other societies. Why would we want to think that way? Besides, comparison and contrast in our thinking limits cooperation and, in the long run, cooperation is of much more value to us for our happiness, survival, and the good of the planet. These ways of thinking are just not worth it.

Because Native people do not naturally use these forms of thinking, there is no concern about straight or gay, for example. Each person is made by the Creator, the Creator doesn't make mistakes, and the Creator likes variety (just look around you!). So, we honor each as created. It's that simple.

Native people tend not to think in a way that is based on assumptions. Assumptions are usually based on disembodied thinking and are not very valuable. The twelve-step program of Alcoholics Anonymous states that assumptions are preconceived resentments. Think about it.

How often do you get angry because of preconceived assumptions you have thought up?

Is it worth it?

Participating in the Process of Native Thinking

Native thinking is very complex and tends to process a great variety of information simultaneously.

Our forms of thinking include body awarenesses, information from our unconscious, whisperings from our dreams, intuition, hunches, signs, flashes, "knowings," feelings, and even "messages" that come in many forms.

Often our most important information will come in the form of a feeling.

For example, as a Native person, one of my survival mechanisms has been to know when I am being lied to.

Usually my thinking or my brain are not my best methods to detect dishonesty. I really want to believe people and I want to believe that I can trust them, and this affects my brain. My first indication that someone is being dishonest with me comes from my solar plexus. I have learned that when I get a "twinge" in my solar plexus, I am usually being lied to, and I am always better off if I pay attention to that twinge. I usually don't know what I am being lied to about, and I can get in trouble if I start trying to figure out specifics. I also get in trouble if I jump on this twinge too soon. Whatever it is, it probably is not what my mind jumps to. I need to pay attention to my twinge and wait with more information. I have often found that Native "thinking" amounts to waiting for more information. It will come.

Often, in Native thinking, our job is *not* to think. For example, in much or most of my writing, I find my most satisfying writing comes when I am not thinking. If I am thinking too much, I need to take a break. Sometimes (quite often), we are not ready to know something. We can't know more than we are ready to know. That's just the way it is. Knowing often comes slowly, at surprising moments, and we have to wait with the process.

Mr. Kelly, the Australian Aboriginal elder who spent so much time with me, used to tell me a lot of stories over and over as elders sometimes do. Sometimes my attention would falter.

"I've heard that story," I would tell myself and relax a bit.

Then, he would throw in something new, which would wake me up.

Over time, I learned that he was feeding me information as I was ready to hear it, and he was a good judge of when I was able to hear it.

With all Native elders, learning is a process, not an event.

Our job is never to assume that we have learned enough. We need to keep open to new information. When we are open-minded, we don't have agendas. Agendas limit what we might learn.

We always have all sorts of information coming at us. Our job is not to "think" about it. Often I know more than I think I know because I have so many pieces of information flowing around from so many sources that I haven't "categorized" yet and am not ready to use. Thinking will cause me to think I know more than I do.

I need to let my unconscious filter and be willing to let pieces flow out when they will. Often in my writing, I am surprised at what comes out on the page. My best writing is always when I am not "thinking" about it.

We need not to start with our brains. Our job is to let in as much information as possible, to integrate it, and to understand it with our whole being—not just our brain. The information takes many forms—intuition, body sensations, *ahas*—and then is put together in our brain. Leading with the brain is not the Native way to think.

It's our brains that keep us in the past ("If only . . . ") and take us to the future ("What if . . . ..."). Our old ones did not indulge in this kind of thinking. I know it is difficult for minds trained in the dominant culture to imagine that Native people did not spend their time regretting the past or fearing the future. And, they didn't.

The Native thinking we came out of is wedded with an *acceptance* of what is. Pre-worry is not part of the Native world. This kind of thinking participates in and trusts the process of the universe. It is not always struggling to change and impose itself upon the Creator's creation. The issue is to live with all that is given with gratitude. Like everything else, our ability to think is—a gift of the Creator. We are not to abuse it.

As Chief Joseph of the Nez Perce said: "I am not a child—I can think for myself. No man can think for me."

Descartes said, "I think, therefore I am." The Native person would find that statement confusing as in our world we are not defined by our thinking.

Instead of "I think, therefore I am," my great-grandmother might say—"I suppose, Elizabeth Anne, we might say, yes, 'I am' and more importantly 'The All' is."

She always had her priorities in fine order.

The Seventeenth Process

Patience

PATIENCE IS TRUSTING THE PROCESS OF GOD.

I always say that I was born an Aries and patience isn't my strong suit.

I am the kind of person that has a hundred irons actively in the fire and another two hundred warming up to go into the fire.

I have *learned* patience and am very grateful for that process. Patience makes life much easier.

Native people the world over have waited for Western culture to discover that in the spiritual growth of the human species we have taken a long detour with mechanistic science, materialism, and technology—now, that's patience.

I have described the way my great-grandmother used to get me ready for bed. She personified patience.

For me, patience comes from a deep knowing that I am part of a greater whole and trusting that the Creator is wiser than I am, sees a greater picture, and is in charge. There is a kind of ease and security in knowing that everything is in the process of unfolding and if I just participate in that process, I don't really need to know where it is going or what will happen because I can't know.

It's just that easy. I can't know. And, knowing that I can't know is a great comfort. I really don't need to know when I participate.

When I was little, I loved being with and watching my great-grandmother. She sewed all her clothes by hand.

I can see her in her cane-backed rocking chair—you know the kind, with wide wooden arms. She would sit there sewing as she slowly rocked back and forth. There seemed to be no deadline to when she needed to finish the dress. She would sew awhile, take a break, sew some more, put it in her lap awhile and rest her eyes—have a cup of tea with me—and slowly the dress and everything else would progress.

She took the same care when she was preparing "medicines" for people who needed them. We would go out picking herbs and digging roots together. She wouldn't always stop at the first plant of the type she wanted when we found it. Often, she would send me ahead "scouting"—after she had taught me what to look for. All too often for me, the first or second or third plant of the type we wanted would not be "right" and so sometimes we spent hours looking for the "right" plant—the one that was just right for the person who needed help. She patiently helped me try to see what the differences were in the same kind of plant.

When she mixed and prepared the medicine—whether it was a tea, a poultice, a powder, or something to put on the food, she always worked with such patience and such care that, in the end, I, without question, knew that whatever she had prepared for the person would, indeed, be healing, even if just because of the way she prepared it.

Often, I sat in on her sessions with people who came to her for "doctoring." They all knew me anyway. Yet, she would always say, "This is Elizabeth Anne. She is my assistant. You feel all right with her being here, don't you?"

I never remember anyone saying that they were not comfortable with my being there. They always seemed comfortable with whatever. I knew that there were many times I "heard things" that usually would not have been said in front of someone my age, and Grandma and the person talking seemed to think it was all right since I was her assistant.

After the person left, we would never talk about her or him. I could ask Grandma questions about what she gave them or why she did what she did. She always patiently dealt with every question.

Sometimes I would ask her why she let someone go on and on about something.

"Well, Elizabeth Anne, sometimes people just need to talk. If we are willing to listen long enough, they may say what they need to hear."

I wonder if this is why I spent so many years as a psychotherapist. Certainly the patience she taught me served me well. It was just that Western psychology was the wrong paradigm for me to be working out of.

I almost never heard Grandma use the word *patience* in reference to herself. She just personified it.

I have come to believe that patience is directly related to a complete trust in all creation, one's place in that creation, and that life will unfold in a way that is in keeping with the process of God.

We may not always understand what that process is or how it works, and if we just trust it, more will be revealed. Always, more will be revealed if we do not let our thinking and our assumptions get in the way.

Knowing our place and knowing we have a place evolves into patience.

To repeat what the Irish elder from Ballinafad, County Galway, Ireland, said to me: "God made time and He made plenty of it." The Irish know a bit about patience too.

When I think of what my people have endured—colonization, the Trail of Tears, discrimination, poverty, abuse, discounting, and the pretense that we and our culture no longer exist—and still we survive, I am sure that patience must be in our DNA or we would not be here.

Participating in the Process of Patience

"Remember, Elizabeth Anne, anything worth doing is worth doing well," my mother always said.

How patient the McCoy women and elder girls were when we went to visit them and they took down the stretched quilt in the rack in the living room. The rack was always there with a quilt project on it. It was simple—just four sticks of wood nailed into a rectangle with each corner held up by a heavy twine "rope." The rope was wound around the piece of wood at each corner to lower and raise the stretched fabric that was being quilted. The pattern had already been drawn on the quilt and all we had to do was sit around, chat, and quilt.

I can remember how proud I felt being able to sit with the ladies and older girls and quilt together. I was always patiently given instructions and praised on my work. I don't think I was very good, and I tried hard. Years later, I wondered if they took out my stitches after I left. I don't think so. They had invested so much time in patiently showing me just how to make the small even stitches that were a challenge for my little fingers. I really don't think they took my stitches out because, years later, they would show me the quilt and we would all laugh about my "stitches" since I was the youngest of the crowd and all. Teasing was always a part of the patience.

It is difficult to be patient in today's world. Everyone is in such a rush.

And, practicing patience is almost as crucial as honoring elders when it comes to participating in "being" Native.

As you go through your daily life, try to look for opportunities to practice the process of patience.

There are few behaviors that will link you to the wisdom of your ancestors so quickly as patience.

We need to practice patience to wait with our knowings.

We need to practice patience to hear those kinds of information that choose not to use our brains as their vehicle of choice.

We need to use patience even to be around elders—much less to be open to what they are saying to us.

We need to have patience to live our spirituality and participate in it as fully as possible.

We need to have patience to participate in the process of our lives.

We cannot *decide* to be patient. Patience has to season us.

The Eighteenth Process

Humility

OUR ANCESTORS PRACTICED a form of humility that is particular to our worldview.

In fact, humility is a natural outcome of our worldview. Our ancestors had such a clear knowing that they were a given part of something bigger than themselves. They knew that their place was a gift and a given fact. They knew that they did not earn that place and they were not entitled to their place. In fact, entitlement was never an issue to be considered as everything they had and everything that came to them was a gift of the Creator. To feel entitlement or deserving was an attitude that simply made no sense and did not exist. Humility involves a natural gratitude for all that is so freely given. When one knows that the Creator provides for all her/his needs (not necessarily all the wants that build up in a materialistic/consumer society!), there is a peace and security that emerges that is almost incomprehensible in today's world. Our old ones lived out of the certainty of their place and the givenness of that reality. In such a world, competition for each person's place in the whole made no sense because everyone—no matter what their sexual orientation, no matter if they were "different" in some way, no matter who or what they were, each had a place and made a valuable and unique contribution to the whole.

It is very difficult for anyone born into today's dominant culture to let the profoundness of the Native acceptance of this reality sink in deep enough to live out of it.

Imagine not having to fight for your place. Imagine having your uniqueness not only quietly accepted but also supported. Imagine the calmness of not having to deal with the institutions of celebrity and royalty.

It is difficult to imagine isn't it?

Yet, our old ones simply knew that they had a place and it was their responsibility to live in that place and participate in it as fully as possible.

How different it is to know that everything—absolutely everything—in all creation is important. How exciting it is to learn about all creation from a perspective of neutrality and participation without having to deal with illusions of entitlement, hierarchy, superiority, or unbelonging.

Our old ones knew that they belonged, they had their place, and that they were not lesser than or better than anyone or anything else. What a relief! How much time this attitude toward life gives for spiritual development, fun, art, storytelling, and living.

When I was growing up, my great-grandmother was my model for so much of living life. I can see now that she was an important person in our little community since so many people came to her to get help and direction in their healing. She, of course, was very important to me, and I was very lucky to be able to tend to and care for her as she was older than anyone else I knew. And, as I look back, the humility and grace with which she moved through life were so amazing and impressive.

She was clearly the reigning elder in our household, and when guests came, she, my mother, and I waited until everyone else had been served before we ate. If we suspected that there might not be enough food for everyone, we took very small portions so our guests could have plenty. We did not want to embarrass them by not eating at all. That would not have been good. And, we knew our place. Our focus was to see that they felt honored and respected as guests and were given everything we could provide so that they would be happy, satisfied, comfortable, and at ease. I never, ever got the feeling that we were sacrificing anything.

No false humility of "see how good I am" ever entered my world as a child. As I grew older and ventured into the larger world, I found myself struggling with the behavior and the concept I later identified as false humility. False humility can only exist in a world where one does not know that she/he has a secure, given place that is part of the process of a greater whole.

The other most humble person I have known was Frank Fools Crow. Grandpa Fools Crow so clearly knew that he worked for the Creator and had his place in that work. His humility was such a given that there was never even a word for it. Humility was an unstated state of his being. When one is at one's best, a hollow bone for the Creator, and when one takes no credit at all for the work he does, humility pervades. There is simply no place for ego, self-importance, or self-centeredness. Life just is and it is service.

Humility is accepting life as a living process and opening ourselves to every possible learning.

Humility is knowing that if we don't get the learning the first time around, it will keep coming around again and again. It may be a progressively harder whack until we notice it, and it will keep recycling until we get it. Can you see the security, relief, and peacefulness in that knowing?

Humility is knowing that there is more than we can ever understand and accepting that truism with joy and relief.

Humility is knowing that there is a purpose behind everything and our job is to trust our knowing.

Humility is softness and service.

Humility is trusting that we will know more as we need to know more.

Humility is knowing that we are part of a much larger whole and that all are important to that whole.

Humility is getting so lost in God's process that everything seems easy.

False humility smarts.

Participating in the Process of Humility

Humility

Humility is
Happiness
Taking a breath
Not a
long breath -
Just a breath
Between
and among
what
comes next

Humility is
not a thought
It is a state
of being
Which comes
easier with
Life's knocks and
age

The Nineteenth Process

Prayer

ALL LIFE, ALL ACTION, all being is an act of prayer.

For the Native person life is lived with everything being a possibility for prayer.

Waking up is approached as an opportunity for prayers of gratitude for the sleep, for the new day, for renewal itself, for the sun rising, for the opportunity of a new day, for life itself. Life is lived as an attitude of prayer.

A Tsa La Gi greets the day at sunrise and goes to the waters to bathe, washing away the shadows of the sleep and the night. Starting the day with the waters is more than a refreshing dip in the stream, lake, bath, or shower. Starting the day with a "cleansing" is an act of prayer. It is a way of respecting and honoring our bodies as gifts from the Creator to be kept healthy. My people have never been able to understand people who did not bathe and/or sweat at least two times a day, and not to start the day with cleansing was incomprehensible.

One of my Cherokee elders told me that I should always remember that brushing my teeth was an opportunity for prayers. I should brush my teeth with an attitude of prayer and when I spit out the toothpaste and rinse my mouth with water, it should be an act of letting go of poisons and resentments I had been holding on to, so I could come to the Creator fresh and peaceful.

For the Native person, life is lived as a prayer of gratitude, and special opportunities for prayer present themselves throughout the day and throughout our lives.

My "sister," a very dear and beloved friend and relative who lived on the Colville Reservation in Washington State, always used to visit me at Boulder Hot Springs in Montana. This place was much loved by the First people of that area. It was always considered a place of ceremony, healing, and trading, and even tribes who usually had hostilities for one another would not fight there. The First Peoples called the area Peace Valley. A group of us have bought the old place and are perpetually restoring the old inn while we heal the wetlands and the land. We are dedicated to its being a place for gathering, healing, rejuvenation, and restoration. Very early on it became clear that the people could not heal unless the building and the land were healed. The building could not heal unless the people and the land were healed, and the land could not heal unless the building and the people were healed. Very shortly after we made that decision, a white bear (which represents much the same meaning as the white buffalo does in other places) was seen at the edge of the property. Since then, the birds and the animals have returned to that place in greater number.

My sister from the Colville Reservation told me many stories of that place where she had come as a child. Every time she came, we would clear the hot pools, and she and I would go into the hot pools and do "prayers and ceremony" in the waters. She would sing her song and we gave thanks for the healing waters.

She always said, "Pray to the waters, give thanks for the healing of the waters. Talk with the waters. Ask for their healing. Show them how much you appreciate them. Ask the waters for help. The waters are very powerful. They will help you." She lived to be well into her nineties, and going into the waters to pray, showing gratitude, and asking for help were all important to her until her death. She always brought gifts to the waters and the steam room. Until she died, she dug roots and gathered healing herbs for all of us, to help remind us how much the earth cared for us and how much we needed, prayerfully, to return the favor.

She always said, "Ask the waters for help for anything you need. They will help you."

As a Tsa La Gi, I have always found it more difficult to ask for help from the Creator than I have to constantly give prayers of gratitude.

As a child, I was taught to "do my part" in all the workings of the world that were presented to me. I also knew that as I worked hard, always willing to serve and do my part, that I would be doing what I could do to honor the Creator and honor all creation. Asking for help was all right, and I never should ask for help for frivolous things or selfish things. Usually, one asked for help for things that had to do with the greater good.

As a Tsa La Gi, I was taught to have a relationship with the Creator. I worked with the Creator for the good of all creation. This was the Tsa La Gi way of *living* prayer; this was the way it was. Getting what I wanted was not the Creator's issue. Getting what I needed was the Creator's issue and I could rest in that confidence. I was grateful for my health and strong body with which I could be of service. So, for me, asking the waters for help always, by definition, took the form of asking the Creator to give me the strength and wisdom to do the work of the Creator. The smaller, more selfish things, I needed to take care of myself—that is just the way I was taught. Prayer should not be abused, especially for the material.

As I said earlier, I was told by one Tsa La Gi woman elder that we Cherokee do not bow our heads when we pray. (To be a strong woman— a strong person—is expected of a Tsa La Gi.) "God likes us to face her/him straight on," she would say. After years of Christian training, it has not been easy for me to always "look God in the eye," and I can see the value in this. Humility is not bowing our heads and closing our eyes. Humility is knowing our place. I am reminded of one of my favorite hymns as a child—"In the Garden":

> *I come*
> *to the garden*
> *alone,*

while
the dew
is still
on the roses,
and the voice I hear,
falling
on my ear,
the Son of God
discloses

And
He walks with me
And
He talks with me
And he tells me
I am his own
And the joy we share
As we tarry there
None other
Has ever
Known

That pretty well sums up this Tsa La Gi woman's relations with God. Respect and honor, intimacy and cooperation.

We work together for all creation. When I don't do that, I'm off track. It's that simple.

So, prayer, for the Native person, is a way of living—a way of being in the world not of the world.

There are specific times for prayer in addition to *living* prayer.

We, of course, pray before meals. We are so grateful to have been given such good food from our Mother, the Earth, and we are so grateful to the hands that prepared it. We need, always, to acknowledge those who do so much for us and make our lives so much easier and better. This focus, of course, just makes good common sense.

Christians, of course, have made their prayers much more complex (and longer!). Worship, praise, thanksgiving, intercession—a whole list of elements. We Native people don't care as much about covering all the bases and why should we bother the Creator too much? We can do better by serving the Creator and all creation with a prayerlike life. It just seems simpler for us all.

It is good to ask for open hearts and open minds before every meeting. We need to hear these words on a regular basis. It is also good to settle down and remind ourselves that we are always in the presence of the Creator and all creation and should act accordingly with honor and respect. This attitude just makes sense to a Native person.

For a Native person, admitting our wrongs and righting them are also forms of prayer and may give the Creator a chuckle.

In fact, I have often wondered if the Creator did not create human beings for pure amusement.

The trees know what they are supposed to do and they do it.

The animals know what they are supposed to do and they do it.

Humans seem to forget what they are supposed to do and keep trying to figure out "better" and "easier" ways to do what we are supposed to do and, as a result, get ourselves in terrible messes along the way. This is how and why we developed technology before we were spiritually ready. I am just sure at times, the Creator can't help but laugh uproariously. Hopefully the plants and animals and the Earth Mother are praying for us.

Participating in the Process of Prayer

When we do not separate prayer from our lives, it is easier to pray and our lives are easier.

Practice living as prayer.

The Twentieth Process

The Unseen

MUCH OF THE WORLD OF OUR ANCESTORS was informed by the unseen.

It is just as my mother said to me, "Always remember, Elizabeth Anne, the unseen is more important than the seen."

We live in a world in which the prevailing belief system is based on a science that discounts and almost completely denies the unseen. This religious/scientific worldview tells us that if something cannot be registered by the senses or an extension of the senses (microscope, telescope, etc.), measured, and controlled, it does not exist. In other words, we need only concern ourselves with the material plane and nothing exists beyond, beside, or in addition to the material planes. This particular scientific worldview also tells us that nothing exists beyond, or parallel with, what the methodology of that particular scientific method can validate and handle.

This scientific belief system is very good for dealing with the material plane and mechanics and technology. Unfortunately, it has not proved to be very effective with the more important processes of life and spirituality.

Centuries ago, some of our European ancestors made a deal that the "new" science could be in charge of the science, mechanics, and technology if it left spirituality to the Church. This "agreement" has not worked out very well for humans, animals, plants, the earth as a whole, or our spiritual growth and development.

The science and spirituality of our Native ancestors went from the particular to the whole and back again and was based on wholeness and process and was, I believe, better for all concerned.

They recognized that a large majority of the influences in our world were in the realm of the unseen and yet were very active in our lives. Although we cannot see these forces, we can see their effects. Concurrently, persons trained to see the unseen, and who have not closed their minds to the unseen, "see" more than what those who are untrained can see.

Our old ones knew that our world was inhabited by ghosts, spirits, "little people," goblins, earth spirits, and many more forces and processes than we ever knew.

In Ireland, the people still talk about the choice of those of the old fairy religion deciding to go underground or into other dimensions in the violent face of Christianity, disappearing until it's safe to come out again. The old fairy rings still exist and one who is open-minded can learn a lot about a different world if that person is willing to go sit in one of those old fairy rings long enough.

When my mother was a young woman, she was known as a ghost hunter. She knew there were such things as ghosts. She had seen and talked to some and she also knew there were "imaginings" going on to scare people and discredit the reality of ghosts. So, she and a few of her colleagues would go to places that were supposed to be haunted or where ghosts were supposed to be and explore and collect data as to the reality of ghosts and "hauntings." Many times she uncovered hoaxes, and sometimes she discovered actual ghosts.

I remember one specific time when I was with her on one of her ghost-hunting excursions. I was about six years old at the time and have very clear and vivid memories of the whole adventure. My great-uncle Bud and his wife, Ruby, were interested in buying a farm down in southern Oklahoma and invited us to go with them to look the property over.

The property had a house that hadn't been lived in for some time and included several hundred acres of farmland. It was on the market for a good price. The owner said that there was no electricity or water and we were welcome to camp there if we wanted, in order to get a feel for the place. We all set out on an exciting adventure. We arrived midafternoon, walked around a bit—I remember getting caught on the barbed wire fence and getting a rather nasty cut—and set up camp not far from the house. Clearly, it had been a beautiful house. It was built off the ground about three feet as was common in that part of the country because it tended to be damp. The house was a large two-story with a big porch wrapping it on all four sides. There would be plenty of room for Grandma and us to visit or even live there if we wanted.

We ate an early supper around the campfire, and as it was starting to get dusk—we have lingering twilights in that part of the country—my uncle and Ruby decided that they should drive over and let the owners know that we had arrived. Mother and I were tired, and we were enjoying the campfire, so we decided to stay.

After dark, Mother and I were sitting by the fire when, all of a sudden, this huge banging noise started up. I was scared, but Mother said not to be afraid, that it would probably be something easily explained. We had my uncle's revolver and my mother's nine-cell flashlight, so we were quite fine. Mother said that we would investigate and that could be fun. She seemed quite calm at that time. I grabbed her hand, glued myself to her side, and "decided" to be calm, although the pit of my stomach did not come along quite as easily. The noise was loud and scary. There would be a very loud BANG, BANG, BANG, BANG, and then SILENCE. Just when I began to relax, the banging would start all over again. It seemed to come from one place and then another.

"What is it, Mother?" I kept asking.

"I don't know," she would whisper. "Maybe it is a cow rubbing against a loose board on the siding," she suggested.

With the pistol strapped on her side and the flashlight in her hand, we crept around the house—no loose boards, no cattle, nothing under the house. When we went up on the porch, it sounded like the noise was coming from the outside and when we went down on the ground, it sounded like the noise came from within the house.

Mother investigated and investigated, with my saying, "Let's go, *please*." She was sure she could find a natural reason. We did not.

At some point, I could tell that her rational mind had exhausted all its resources and her knowledge of the unseen took over.

"This is not a benevolent entity," she said. We are leaving.

"Do not turn your back on it, Elizabeth Anne. Walk slowly with me down the lane while I keep the gun and the flashlight turned on the house."

It was very dark now, and when we reached the road we started walking in the direction we thought my aunt and uncle had gone. After what seemed to me to be a very long time, a pickup truck approached. Mother turned on the flashlight so they could see us and not hit us. Mother tended to wear jodhpurs and high-laced English boots when we went out in the woods because of the snakes. She loved snakes and even collected rare specimens for the St. Louis Zoo. We actually had trapped an unusual spreading adder earlier that day that we were taking back with us. She always said it was safer to wear high boots so as not to tempt fate. I was in my cowboy boots.

The two young men said that they stopped because when they saw the silhouette of her jodhpurs and boots. They thought it was the highway patrol and maybe the bridge was washed out. They were surprised to see a woman and a child. When we told them where we were going, they turned the truck around and gave us a ride.

Mother told them that my aunt and uncle were thinking about buying the farm that was for sale. Everything suddenly stopped—even the breathing. The young men were visibly shaken.

"Were you two there alone after dark?" one stammered.

"Yes," said Mother. "Why?"

They both began talking at once. Their story was that they had been offered jobs from the previous owner and been told they could stay at the house. They were scared to death even talking about it. They said they would never go near it again no matter how much anybody paid them. They had heard the same sounds and never had been able to see where they came from.

As we drove up, my uncle and aunt were surprised to see us and the two young men.

When the six of us talked with the "new owners," it seemed that they had bought their current farm and the other one sight unseen. When they got down there, they could see that the two farms were too much for them so they had put the one we were looking at on the market. According to the owner, this was the first time they had heard about the "noises."

We went back to the house that night. We pried the boards off and went into the house. We investigated every aspect of the house, checking out one theory that the sound was like someone had been stomping up and down the stairs. The dust was undisturbed on the stairs. We boarded ourselves in one room, one person kept guard all night with the light on. We left the next morning. My aunt and uncle did not buy that farm.

I remember my mother's words, "Don't be afraid of the unseen, Elizabeth Anne. Don't doubt that it exists. Don't ignore it. Understand it as much as you can. Work with it."

In my family, we lived with and explored all aspects of our world, the seen and the unseen, as best we could. I learned that there are many things we do not understand. That is as it should be. Just because we do not understand them does not mean they are not there.

We can't see radio waves, microwaves, or the magnetic lines that band the earth, but they exist and affect us. Western science has now come to accept their existence because it has learned to measure them with its instruments. How much more is there that Western science has not yet learned to detect that still affects us?

I knew a world-famous psychic who was also an MD. He was raised and trained in a very traditional way. Then, at one point in his medical career, he had a case in which he was working with a woman who inexplicably would show up at his office with symptoms. Yet, all the medical tests indicated that she should not be having these symptoms. After much research, he discovered that she had an identical twin who lived almost a thousand miles away. Whenever her twin became ill, she came down with the same symptoms even when she had no information that her twin was ill. That experience launched his research into the world of the unseen.

He was open-minded and willing to research the unseen and the unknown. He was not limited by the assumptions, worldview, and methodology with which he grew up and in which he was trained.

Being open-minded means that we are open to all knowledge and information. Native science in its wholeness can handle all kinds of information and data.

There are people who talk with the spirits who say that they are trying to help us. Why wouldn't our DNA hold the possibility of all kinds of information from our ancestors?

Just because some of us have not become sophisticated enough to detect the unseen is not proof that it does not exist.

There are ghosts, spirits, "little people," goblins, and earth spirits that regularly make themselves known to some people. If our science and the resultant pollution of our minds and our earth do not kill everything off, perhaps they will help us with the problems we now face.

Maybe one of the reasons we need the wisdom of the Native worldview right now is because the Native people have kept a relationship with and knowledge of the unseen. Who knows?

I know in my own life I have always been open to all experiences and understandings. As a result, I have witnessed and experienced phenomena that Western science just cannot handle.

I was privileged to know the Cherokee and Shoshone medicine man Rolling Thunder who, like most medicine people, was able to deal with the unseen quite readily. A reliable story is told about him by a man who witnessed his ability to deal with the unseen. This man was driving Rolling Thunder to a meeting. At one point, Rolling Thunder realized that he had forgotten his pipe bag. He made clear that he wanted to have it with him. He then fell silent and appeared to doze. According to his driver, the bag and pipe were suddenly in his lap. I have seen many instances of a similar nature by people I consider to have an open connection with the Creator—they are able to be a hollow bone. There were always many spirits and other entities present when Fools Crow did a ceremony. He could always call on the White Stone healers when he needed them to heal others.

When I first met Rolling Thunder, I did not know who he was and was standing behind him waiting to talk with the person with whom he was conversing. Suddenly, he wheeled on me and, with his piercing blue eyes, looked deep into me. He had felt me. He then said, "Oh, you're not here to be healed. You're one of the healers. We need to talk. Meet me for breakfast tomorrow. I need to teach you."

How could I refuse?

People who are open-minded and in touch with the unseen have a broader range of phenomena from which to choose than those who are bound by rigid beliefs. These people also have a responsibility to use these gifts wisely, for the good of all creation.

Dreams are one door to the unseen that is available to all of us. In my experience, it is best not to get our thinking minds involved and thus try to interpret our dreams. Rarely are meaningful dreams linear and logical. Yet, if we honor our dreams and wait with the process of becoming clear with them, they can give us important information.

When my mother was a young woman, she had a horse she loved very much, Brownie. During the Depression, she had to sell her horse. As a result of this forced sale, much of my early childhood was spent looking for Brownie. At last we found her, and the horse and my mother were able to live out Brownie's last years together. Clearly, they had a special connection. I have always been taught that animals are necessary in our lives as teachers and that they teach us things we could not otherwise learn so easily. Brownie was one of my teachers and she taught me well.

After Brownie died, she would come to my mother in dreams. My mother would always see her on the side of a green hill whinnying to her. Mother would always be off-center and disturbed by these dreams. Over the years, we came to see that when Mother had a "Brownie dream" our lives were going to be terribly shaken up in some way. Even my "scientific" father came to walk on eggshells when Mother had a Brownie dream. There would be a death of a relative or close friend, or Daddy (who worked for the US government) would get transferred to another part of the country. Something always happened within a few days of the dream that disrupted our lives over which we had no control. All of us came to believe in Mother's "Brownie dreams." We had the data.

There are so many aspects to the unseen that I feel pushed to write about a wide range of these phenomena. People who have these experiences often have been treated as if they are crazy by the dominant, closed-minded culture, and they have taken this judgment in.

Years ago, just after I had written my first book, *Women's Reality*, I went to visit an old friend who was a psychoanalyst in New York City. I wanted to visit with her and present her with my book. She was pleased with the visit and the book and, after a while, she said, "You've changed!"

"Well, I hope so," I said. "We haven't seen each other for a few years, and I hope I haven't been static," I said with a chuckle.

"No, I'm serious," she said. "You have really changed."

I settled down. Psychoanalysts are always serious, especially when they are giving a free observation.

"You no longer think you are crazy," she said quite seriously.

I was a bit shocked.

"Did I think I was crazy before?" I asked, a bit off-center.

"Yes," she said—again quite seriously.

I sat with this startling new information for a few minutes.

"Well, now I know I am, in the eyes of the culture, and I feel just fine with it," I said with a true Cherokee twinkle in my eye.

We both relaxed into my new perfectly facilitated "insight" and went on chatting.

She knew me well—and I her—and we have always been good friends. We are very different in most ways—which is good.

Participating in the Process of the Unseen

I have had many experiences of the unseen being active in my life. For example, I really don't like to fly, and I especially dislike turbulence. Many years ago, I was flying from Denver to Wichita, Kansas, to give a speech. I had just received a manuscript on which I needed to do the final editing before I left for Europe. My time on the plane was the only time I had to work on it before I went overseas, and I had a deadline.

Upon boarding the plane, I settled in and started right to work. Then, I noticed that the flight attendants were serving the meal before the drinks were served and I asked why.

"Some pretty bad turbulence has been reported ahead of us and the pilot has told us to get the meal service out of the way before it gets too bad."

I was furious! Here I am writing these books and making these speeches, flying overseas, and trying as best I can to do what I think the Creator wants, and I am going to have too much turbulence to edit. Something was really *wrong*. At the first bump, I mentally said, "Spooks"—that's my fond intimate term for my spirit guides—"if you want me to do this work, I need a little help here. If I'm not on the right track, I'll just bump around and hate it."

Immediately, the air cleared, we had a very smooth ride, and I was able to get almost all of the manuscript proofread on that flight. As we landed, the pilot came on and said, "Folks, welcome to Wichita. Every plane before and after us has reported severe turbulence, and we had a smooth ride. I don't understand it, and I'm glad for us all that that is the way it was." I smiled seraphically to myself.

This experience on airplanes has now become a regular occurrence, and almost always the captain comes on and gives some similar message. I am just grateful, and I keep trying to do the Creator's work.

I have many and varied experiences with my "spooks" and know that I am guarded over and have lots of help.

Much of my writing is a surprise to me and I feel free to say that I really like the way it comes out sometimes, because it does not feel like it is "mine."

I often have "conversations" with Frank Fools Crow, my great-grandmother, my mother, or others when I need them. I have begun to believe that the beginning of turbulence on a plane is Fools Crow's way of "ringing me" for an important discussion. Often, the plane ride is the first bit of quiet I have had for a while and a good time for an important "talk."

These are a few of the examples of the unseen in my life and are what I consider to be a natural part of the life I lead.

As long as I am doing my best to do the work of the Creator, I assume I will have what I need—and the wisdom of the unseen is definitely what I need.

So many Native people I meet have had experiences with the unseen, feel crazy, and want to deny and hide their experiences. Don't go there.

I was taught to trust my perceptions as a child, an upbringing which I have since learned is unusual in this culture. Even so, I had taken on some of those distorted ideas that, because of my experiences and open-mindedness, there was something wrong with *me*.

Not so! Remember, in Native cultures differences are an opportunity to be explored and lauded. It's all in the perspective.

On the other hand, it is important not to get "woo woo" with these experiences. My friend, the psychic, calls it "being pooky-pooky." Because we live in a culture that denies the reality of these experiences, when we do have them we might be tempted to see ourselves as special. As in most dualisms, both ends are dangerous.

Just let the experiences be. Don't deny or aggrandize them. Just learn from them.

Years ago, I was sitting at the closing dinner for a monthlong workshop I had been facilitating, and suddenly I felt very strange—like I wasn't quite in my body. Then, I left. I could still hear the people talking where I was physically and, simultaneously, I "came in" in another time and another place. I was in a Scottish or Irish village in the last century. My first thought was that I should look around and see who I knew in that place. I loved the feeling of being "disembodied"—no aches—no pains—no stress. There was a fair in the village and much happening. I clearly "belonged" there. After a while, I reluctantly decided to return to the people at the dinner who were yelling at me and shaking me. The first thing I said on my return was that I had been somewhere else. No one was interested. No one at the hospital understood. My children did. For a while, I was concerned that I wouldn't "stay" here, since the feeling of being in that alternate reality was so pleasant and I was so curious.

My children would know when I was starting to "leave." They would say, "Mom's leaving again," and they would get me up and walk me around in the sunshine if possible.

I decided to stay in *this* reality (obviously)—at least for a while.

And, what I experienced and learned was that we can exist in two or more dimensions at the same time.

I had never been able to get my mind around the concept of living parallel lives.

Now, I had experienced it. I trusted my perceptions.

Luckily, I had always been taught to be open-minded, so I checked out and trusted my perceptions. If we distort our experiences—whatever they are—we will not benefit from them. Nor will others.

It is possible to communicate with rocks, trees, and animals. We have teachers everywhere if we can just clear our minds enough to listen.

It is possible, intuitively, to know what is wrong with someone's body even when our logical minds know nothing about the condition. We get information from somewhere else. This happens all the time if we are open to many sources of information and are not self-centered or gullible.

Whatever information we get from wherever—we always need to check it out in as many ways as we can.

Open-mindedness does not equate with gullibility and self-serving imagination.

If we are given the gifts of the unseen, we are also given the responsibility to check out the information with every means at our disposal.

Just because we are gifted does not mean that we are automatically right.

On the other hand, most of us know a lot more than we think we know. We have more potential than we are willing to let in, and there is much more help and information out there than the dominant culture has been willing to admit and benefit from.

We, as Native people, have a responsibility to use our gifts wisely. Remember, just because we have more information than some people does not mean we are crazy. We just have to learn to use it for the good of all.

The Twenty-First Process
Living in Balance

WE ARE HERE TO MAINTAIN AND CREATE BALANCE. It is as it should be that we move away from balance for we are alive, and we need to learn. Yet, we need to focus our energies on returning to balance or moving to a new balance. Our world is very unbalanced right now.

For living in balance, I would like to return to the teachings of my Cherokee (Tsa La Gi) elders, who told me that there were four things a Cherokee had to do in this life.

1. Honor the Creator
2. Honor all creation
3. Be of service
4. Continue the ceremonies

If we participate in all these four ways of being and acting, we will go a long way toward maintaining and creating balance.

The concept of balance is pretty easy in the dominant, mechanistic, linear culture, which I have in previous writings called the TMM (Technological, Mechanistic, Materialistic culture). This culture is built on stasis and is basically two dimensional. In that worldview, the concept of balance is visualized as a seesaw, and balancing is quite simple, really.

The world of the Native person is not so simple and mechanistic.

The world of the Native person is multidimensional and in a constant process of mutation and change.

The world of the Native person is alive, moving, chaotic, and ordered.

This world is very interesting and very challenging. We really have to step up and be counted to do our job of maintaining and creating balance. Ours is an exciting world in which to participate, and our participation is necessary for this world to grow and flourish in relationship to and with the Creator and all creation.

Participating in the Process of Balance

In the Native way of being, living in balance is not just a concept or an idea. Living in balance is a way of participation in all aspects of our reality.

For Native people, it is very clear that the Creator is in charge. We do not confuse ourselves with being the Creator or being in charge.

It is our responsibility to relate fully to the Creator and see the role of the Creator in every aspect of our lives. To live in balance with the Creator, we need to take responsibility for our relationship with the Creator. We may not always understand the ways of the Creator and we need to accept that reality while respectfully seeking a better understanding and a closer relationship. Living in a state of gratitude with the knowledge that all we have is a gift from the Creator helps a great deal.

Living in balance means that we try to keep our relationship with the Creator clean. Humility, respect, gratitude, and acceptance are ways in which we can honor and keep balance with the Creator. We need to accept that we, as humans, cannot and will not ever understand everything there is to know about the Creator, and it is our responsibility to maintain a living balance with this great mystery as much as we can.

Many of the ceremonies and rituals of Native people are ways to remind us to keep a balanced relationship with the Creator. We are, after all, human beings, and we have to be reminded of our place and our responsibilities from time to time. The trees, plants, rocks, and animals don't think so much, so it is easier for them to keep their relationship with the Creator balanced than it is for humans.

When we are able to keep a balance in our relationship with the Creator, our lives run more smoothly.

As Chief Luther Standing Bear once said, "The man who sat on the ground in his tipi meditating on life and its meaning, accepting the kinship of all creatures and acknowledging the unity with the universe of things, was infusing into his being the true essence of civilization."

In order to live in balance, we need to participate in honoring all creation and care for all creation.

For example, we need to see that we live in balance with our bodies. Our bodies, whatever they are, are a gift from the Creator and we need to honor them as such. Being obsessed with our bodies is not living in balance with our bodies. To live in balance with our bodies, we need to care for them as a gift of the Creator. Overeating bad foods or starving ourselves is not a way to live in balance with our bodies. As we respect our bodies as living manifestations of the Creator, we approach them with grace and dignity. We honor them and seek ways to accept what they are, be in living communication with them, avoid contaminating them with our "thinking" about how or what they should be, listen to them, and try to live a balanced life with them. In doing so, we also honor the Creator and contribute to living in balance with the Creator.

A very important aspect of living in balance is living in balance with our relationships. Although we Native people are very generous and like to give to others, we need to keep a balance in our relationships with others and relate with others who know about keeping balance in relationships.

This may be one of the biggest mistakes our ancestors made with the newcomers when they came to this land. We could see that they needed our help even to survive those early winters. It is true that we did not understand their ways. They had many strange ways and did not seem to know or care about maintaining a balanced relationship with the Creator and all creation. And, it seems that, perhaps, our ancestors assumed too much and did not know how to teach them about balance in their relationships and relationships with all creation. Maybe this kind of balance is what we need to teach now if we can, again, get clear on it ourselves.

One thing is crystal clear, however. We can talk about balance in relationships until the earth disintegrates, but the only way to teach about balance in all relationships, including our relationship with nature, the earth, and the planet is to *do* it—not just talk about it.

I am, by nature, a very generous person. I was, I believe, born that way and I was raised to share what I have. That is just my reality. Yet, over time, I have learned that it is also my responsibility not to let others take advantage of that generosity. I have learned that there are people who will just take and take and take. If I continue to "give" after I have exhausted every possible means I have to bring that relationship into balance, I am contributing to the imbalance in the universe.

For the Native person, it is usually much easier to give and keep on giving than it is to say, "Sorry. Enough! This relationship is out of balance."

Yet, it is our responsibility to establish and maintain balance in all our doings. By not saying "enough," we are then contributing to the imbalance in our personal relationships, with nature and our Mother, the earth, and with the planet. Creating balance in all aspects of our lives is extremely important.

One of the most effective ways I have found for keeping balance in our personal relationships is something that I was taught as a child and then I discovered in a new form in the twelve-step program of Alcoholics Anonymous. AA calls it, "Staying on our own side of the street." The whole process is very simple really and, yet, is quite revolutionary and unusual in today's society.

Whenever there is imbalance in a relationship and things are getting worse and worse, it is important to stop, take a breath, decompress, and get in touch with how we are contributing to the problem. Doing this does not mean that we are to blame; it does not mean that the other person or persons have no responsibility; it does not mean that they are not complete idiots—all this does not matter. If the other persons have been idiots, that is their problem, not ours. Our problem is, quite simply, to see what we have contributed to the imbalance, admit it, and do something to return to balance from our perspective. The surprising thing about this whole process is that, in admitting our part in any imbalance, almost magically our personal power returns, and even if we have done wrong we feel better about ourselves. I have come to believe that this "return of personal power" is because we have acted in such a way as to bring our relationship with the Creator back into balance. This is powerful stuff indeed! Refusing to be a victim or to stay in a state of victimhood allows for the opening of our balanced relationship with the Creator, which is key.

Victims will not heal and *will*, at some point, become perpetrators themselves. It's that simple.

For example, there is no question that our ancestors were used and abused by the visitors who came to stay. What part did they have, and do we have, in perpetrating that abuse and allowing the imbalance between all of us and all of creation to perpetuate and grow?

When we figure this out, we need to admit our part.

Then, the next step is making amends and moving on to balance.

This process is not new to our ancestors and elders. Sitting Bull knew about it when he said, "I was very sorry when I found out that your intentions were good and entirely different from what I supposed they were."

We need to "get on and clean up our side of the street" with respect to our unbalanced relationship with nature, the air, the streams, and our Earth Mother. Allowing unbalanced relationships to continue and "helplessly" contributing to them benefits no one and no part of the creation.

We Native people have a great deal of knowledge about keeping in balance with all of nature and the earth. This knowledge is in our DNA, and it is up to us to live in such a way as to be in balance. We can help teach those who have forgotten how important balance is—balance with all creation.

As my elder taught me, service is essential for creating and maintaining balance. Doing service and being of service is deep in the DNA of every Native person. Service is the vehicle for creating balance. Without service there is no way to return to balance.

I have noticed that whenever I feel off-center, out of touch with the Creator, and out of place with myself, it all disappears if I can find a simple way to be of service. This does not mean that being of service to make myself feel better is the answer. It's not! That is just being self-centered, and we never create balance or feel better for that.

Being of service requires humility and is selfless in nature. As my mother said, "Any decent person would have done the same thing." Being a decent person is being of service. There are so many opportunities to be of service to honor all of creation that we don't have to look far. Simple acts of kindness present themselves everywhere.

It is good to be a giver in our lives and it is also essential to learn to be given to.

Ultimately, it is the balanced flow of energy in, between, and among people that creates balance.

To live in balance is to live a life of ease. Hard work may be involved and, the living is still a life of ease.

Lastly, keeping the ceremonies offers us an opportunity to return to balance.

Ceremonies for Native people are not designed to appease our angry, fearful, and jealous God. That is just *not* how my ancestors experienced the Creator. My ancestors experienced the Creator as gracious, generous, and open to the process of a balanced relationship. Our Creator was one who wanted all creation to heal, grow, expand, and become as full and whole as possible. Our Creator was one who was mystery beyond mystery, and yet participated with us in everyday life, for the growth and expansion of living in balance with all creation. It was all quite simple really.

The ceremonies were not to appease "God." They were to remind *us* of the balance and our place in and responsibility with and to The All. We, as human beings, need to be reminded.

Each culture has its own ceremonies and ways of being in balance with the Creator. It is, therefore, important that we know and perpetuate ours so we can contribute our piece. We do not need to perpetuate our language and culture for the sake of *our* language and culture. We need to keep it alive as an essential part of the whole, so that we can maintain balance within the entirety of the whole. Everyone and every part of creation has a role to play and a responsibility to do so to maintain balance.

The ceremonies and the rituals function best when they are not practiced to perpetuate a certain religion or human dogma. They are best themselves when all approaches are respected and valued, and each adds its piece—however big or small it is—to create balance.

We cannot create balance by believing we are right or that we have the only way. None of us knows that much or has all the pieces. Our rituals and ceremonies are to remind us. Whenever we confuse our piece with the whole, we are not contributing to balance. We are destroying balance. None of us has that luxury.

Open-mindedness creates balance.

Creating balance is the work of every part of creation.

That's just the way it is.

In Summary

Creating a Wholeness of Being

"If the Great and Good Spirit wished us to believe as the whites, he would have changed us."

—Black Hawk (Sauk)

THIS BOOK HAS BEEN WRITTEN TO HELP THOSE who are ready and willing to reawaken and remember a way of being in this world that is spiritually, physically, emotionally, and psychologically balanced and integrated with all creation. It is not intended to impose, control, or require a way of being on anyone. It has been written to support and assist those who are seeking to return to another way that is deeply embedded in their souls.

In order to respond to this longing we will have to be willing to deal with self-imposed and externally imposed prejudices, judgments, and fears.

That's all right. We grow and ripen from dealing with the obstacles that we, ourselves, and others have erected to challenge our resolve. Such is the process of life.

There seems to have been times in the history of the human race when people have emerged to change the course of human history. Sometimes those times have resulted in great leaps of wisdom and spiritual growth. Sometimes these discoveries have not advanced our spiritual growth as a species or a planet and have served as a painful detour that was needed to get us back on track. Sometimes we have just bumbled around wandering in the desert for a while, forgetting how much the Creator has given us and just how precious all creation is.

173

There are many signs that suggest that we have been on a major detour and that our "wanderings" have become so painful for planet earth and the human species that we need to pay attention and somehow return to the wisdom that lies slumbering in each of us—in each of us so that we can, collectively, return to the wisdom to heal the whole.

Clearly, we have distorted the teachings of our elders and lost touch with much of the wisdom buried deep inside us.

We have deluded ourselves into believing that the culture and the wisdom were lost and have felt helpless and despairing.

Yet, our myths and legends have always told us that a time would come when this wisdom would be needed to save the planet, and that time is now.

We were never told that this re-creating would be an easy task. We were only told that it would be the task of those who carried the wisdom. Many of us have felt exempt because we did not know that we had the wisdom buried deep within us. We had tried to deny it all these years.

Slowly a nascent awareness is spreading within many who did not know that they had the seeds of Selu buried deep in their beings and, indeed, have been given the seeds of wisdom that are now needed by us all.

Unfortunately, these seeds cannot sprout unless we are willing to prepare the soil and nourish them with the healing waters.

In order to *be* the fertile soil for the seeds our ancestors planted, we have to do our work to become the kind of people in which these seeds can grow.

There are many aspects to becoming this kind of being.

1. We first have to admit we aren't.
2. We have to *want* to be this kind of being.

3. We have to believe that with the help of the Creator and those around us such change is possible.
4. We have to be willing to shed our cultural and social brainwashing, like the way chelation therapy removes the toxins of heavy metals from our bodies.
5. We have to be ready and willing to ask for help and support.
6. We have to be as open-minded, humble, and receptive as a child.
7. We have to be able to admit and know that we will have all the help we need when we need it if we just do our work and open ourselves to the guidance of our spirit helpers and the Creator.

To accomplish these seven things, we have to be open to the twenty-one processes described in this book (and more—there are many). Then we can serve the Creator in the healing of this planet, and the creatures and life-forms on it.

For our ancestors, this really is not too much to ask. And—the rewards are great.

Like the corn, the seeds have been planted in us, waiting.

This book is to help us respond to the call of our deepest knowings.

This book is to help us respond to the call of our ancestral blood.

The "being" part of each process is the open door.

As the great ancestor, Como, said, "I am opening my heart to speak to you—open yours to receive my words."

> *"Your feet shall be as swift as forked lightning; your arm shall be as the thunderbolt, and your soul fearless."*
>
> —Methoataske (Shawnee)

Pray for us all.

Acknowledgments

THERE ARE SO MANY who have contributed to this book that any listing would, of necessity, be incomplete and inadequate. So, I will mention those who easily come to mind and beg the forgiveness of those not mentioned.

I want to acknowledge and honor the Creator, who constantly and consistently meddles in my life. In spite of this interference, we have a pretty good relationship. This is surprising since, whenever we differ, I am pretty much always wrong about everything, which must say something positive about my character, perhaps.

I want to thank my ancestors for giving me life and accumulated wisdom, feelings, awarenesses, mistakes, and history to season my soul's journey. My parents, grandparents, uncles, and aunties were always teaching me by example how to be, and how not to be, which are all too often difficult to discern except in retrospect.

I want especially to acknowledge Norbert Hill, who offered me the comfort of a sheltering wing of AISES (the American Indian Science and Engineering Society) when I was reaching my bottom with exasperation with respect to dealing with the dominant culture. AISES offered me a place of sanctuary when I most needed it in order to regroup myself.

I want to acknowledge my aunt and uncle, Bow and Phil Lane Sr., Lakota elders and Sioux/Chickasaw spiritual leaders, who with their son, Phil Lane Jr., gave up a vacation at "some rich lady's house in Mexico" to spend their Christmas holiday with us in our little house in Hawaii.

Phil Sr. wanted to pass on his pipe ceremony to me so I could fulfill my responsibility to Frank Fools Crow and the pipe he gave me to carry. Phil Sr. started his teaching at the airport baggage claim and continued through and after the day he died, and still teaches me.

I want to acknowledge the Australian Aboriginal elders who invited me to come to Australia. After they had checked me out—"Why did you come?"

"Because you invited me."

"You aren't doing some kind of research on us for some degree, are you?"

"No, I have two doctorates, and that's enough."

"Then why are you here?"

My answer of "I have no idea" seemed satisfactory, so they then ignored me and my uncontrollable sobbing as I listened to them talk about their lives, their ways, and their issues.

I knew I had found a people who had been able to maintain a "purity" of the real knowledge and understanding that had almost been obliterated in today's world and with them was alive and well.

I especially want to acknowledge Aunt Millie, Australian Koori spiritual leader and keeper of the women's sacred sites in New South Wales, who introduced me to White Buffalo Mountain.

I want to acknowledge the island of Kauai, the 'āina, (the land), and my Hawaiian ohana (family), who tenderly and painstakingly restored my soul and being after years of confused battering by this dominant system. They offered me a healing sanctuary.

I want to acknowledge those who said, "I knew you were Native (Cherokee) from the minute I first laid eyes on you," and eased my journey.

I want to acknowledge the many editors/publishers who have nurtured me over the years to the place where I now recognize when I have an "assignment" to write and, surprisingly, believe that I can do it.

I want to thank those men in my life who love me unconditionally—Pete, my manager, Chuck, my husband, and Roddy, my son. I also want to acknowledge Beth, my daughter, who continues to challenge me, and my grandson, Alexander, who brings Hopi, Castilian Spanish, and Apache ancestral blood into our family. I pray that this book might support him on his life journey.

I want to acknowledge the participants in the International Living in Process network, who continue to let me share my ancestral wisdom with them and challenge me when I get tired or lazy, especially the Pow Wow sub-group, who accept me as their teaching elder, therefore demanding my need to be the very best of what I teach.

I want to acknowledge the Sandra Dijkstra Literary Agency, Jill Marr, my agent, Elisabeth James, and Andrea Cavallaro for their part in bringing this book into being.

I am so honored to have this book published by Council Oak Books, a publisher who has published some of the most important books I have ever read.

Recognizing that my acknowledgements could go on forever, I'll stop now.

It's amazing how everything comes together if we just let the Creator take charge.

Indeed, it's all quite easy really.